So you really want to learn

English

BOOK 1

So you really want to learn

English

BOOK 1

Susan Elkin

Series Editor: Nicholas Oulton M.A. (Oxon.)

www.galorepark.co.uk

Independent Schools
Examinations Board

GALORE PARK

Published by ISEB Publications, an imprint of Galore Park Publishing Ltd,
19/21 Sayers Lane, Tenterden, Kent TN30 6BW
www.galorepark.co.uk

Illustrations by Ian Douglass and Les Garrett

Printed by Cayfosa Quebecor, Spain

ISBN 13: 978 1 902984 53 7

The publishers are grateful for permission to use extracts and photographs as follows: Extract from MELUSINE: © Lynne Reid Banks 1989, reprinted with permission of McIntosh and Otis Inc. Extract from THE MACHINE GUNNERS by Robert Westall by permission of Macmillan Children's Books, London. Extract from KING OF SHADOWS by Susan Cooper published by Bodley Head, used by permission of The Random House Group Limited. Extract from SHADOW OF THE MINOTAUR by permission of the author Alan Gibbons and the publisher Orion Children's Books. Extract from OTHER ECHOES by Adèle Geras published by David Flickling, used by permission of The Random House Group Limited. Extract from I CAN JUMP PUDDLES by permission of the author Alan Marshall and the publisher Penguin Books Australia. Report on the Australia and England rugby match (Chapter 10) by kind permission of the BBC and the website www.news.bbc.co.uk. Extract from BILLY THE KID: Text © Michael Morpurgo (2000), reprinted by permission of Chrysalis Children's Books, a division of Chrysalis Books Group plc. Photograph of the Seychelles by kind permission of the Seychelles Tourist Board. Photographs of elephant in zoo and sea cow by kind permission of Ron Pickering. Photograph of children wearing utility clothing by kind permission of The Mary Evans Picture Library.

First published 2004
Reprinted July 2005, September 2005, July 2007

An Answer Book is available to accompany this book
ISBN 13: 978 1 902984 56 8

Details of other Galore Park publications are available at www.galorepark.co.uk

ISEB Revision Guides, publications and examination papers may also be obtained from Galore Park.

Acknowledgements

Since 1968 I have worked with many thousands of pupils and students of all ages in London, Northamptonshire and Kent. From them I have learned nearly everything I know about how to teach and learn English. In a very real sense this is their book. I thank them all.

I also thank my husband Nicholas Elkin, always the first reader and critic of anything I write. I am indebted to his meticulous eye for detail and his unfailing presence as a sounding board against which I continuously bounce ideas.

Sincere thanks are also due to Nicholas Oulton, my publisher and editor. His business-like, no-nonsense approach makes him a great pleasure to work with. This book owes its existence to his faith in it and in me.

Finally, to Nigel Rammage and his pupils at Papplewick School, Ascot, who kindly 'road-tested' the material in this book, and to Bill Inge of Ashfold School, and Rebecca Connet, leader of the ISEB 13+ English setting team, who both read the proofs with scrupulous care, I give my thanks. I am indebted to them for their enthusiasm and constructive suggestions.

I hope that our combined efforts have eliminated all mistakes. But if any remain they are, of course, mine.

Preface

This book has been written for the Common Entrance Syllabus for examination at 11+. Each chapter is based around two extracts, one literary and the other from a non-literary source, followed by plenty of ideas to get children writing in as many different styles, moods and modes as there are pupils. The ten chapters, with their supplementary focus on spelling, punctuation, grammar, oracy and wider reading, could provide the basis for a whole year's work in English lessons if whole literary texts were studied as a separate, parallel activity. There are extension tasks in every chapter, too, to stretch pupils who finish quickly or who want (or need) to go further.

Examinations are, however, not education. The secondary aim of this book is to develop in children the highest possible standards in English – for its own sake – and to make it pleasurable, rigorous and satisfying. I love English and I want users of this book to learn to love it too.

SJE

Contents

Chapter 4

Chapter 5

Chapter 6

Chapter 7

Introduction

The English Language

The English Language is enormous. It consists of over 500,000 words. Compare that with German which has a vocabulary – or lexicon – of about 185,000 words and French which has fewer than 100,000. Perhaps that's why Shakespeare, the greatest writer, playwright and poet there has ever been anywhere (see Chapter 5) was English. His talents developed partly because of the splendid language he was born into. He couldn't have written in the way that he did in any other language. In fact, you could say that the language produces writers rather than the other way round. Think about that.

So why is English so much larger than other European languages? The reasons lie in our history. When the Romans arrived in Britain under Julius Caesar in 55BC and stayed for over 400 years, they brought Latin. Although most of that disappeared after their final withdrawal in 410 AD, we still have a few words in English, such as 'vinegar', which date from the Roman occupation.

The Romans, as you know from your history, also occupied France. There, Latin took a firmer hold than it had done in England. French developed as a language firmly based on Latin – some of which had developed from Ancient Greek. When William of Normandy and his troops invaded England in 1066, they brought the Latin-based French language with them. Gradually that French got mixed with the language which the native Britons were already speaking. Some people call this old, pre-1066 language Anglo-Saxon, but dictionary makers term it Old English or OE which is really more accurate.

Words from OE include most of the everyday words we use still such as 'went' 'got' 'ate' 'asked' 'spoke' and many thousands of others. New French words from Latin (or occasionally from Greek) tended to be softer, longer and more elegant.

OE	*Originally from Latin via French*
fort	castle
king	sovereign
thought	cogitation
walk	perambulation

So we began to develop a language rich in synonyms (see Chapter 8). We usually have more than one word for things.

By the time Geoffrey Chaucer was writing his famous book *The Canterbury Tales* in the 1390s, Old English had merged fully with French to form a glorious, big, new language which lexicographers – dictionary makers – call Middle English (ME). When Chaucer writes 'He was a verray parfit gentil knight', it isn't too difficult to work out what he means (He was a perfect and very gentle, or genteel, knight).

Fast forward another 200 hundred years to the 1590s and you find Shakespeare writing an early version of modern English – which 21st century readers and listeners can follow quite easily.

Meanwhile words were flowing into English from all over the world because of our long history as seafarers, travellers, explorers, fighters and conquerors. Wherever English people went, for any reason, their language soaked up local words.

The Crusaders (remember Richard the Lionheart?) went to countries at the east end of the Mediterranean Sea in the middle ages to fight for Christianity. Explorers like Walter Raleigh and Francis Drake travelled the world in the 16th century. A century later Captain Cook was sailing round Australia and New Zealand. In Queen Victoria's time David Livingstone and John Speke (see Chapter 7) were the first white men to penetrate parts of Africa.

These are some of the everyday words which have come into English from around the word during the last 1000 years: pyjamas (Persian), parka (Aleutian, an Eskimo or Inuit language), kangaroo (Australian aboriginal), safari (Swahili), wigwam (American Indian), bungalow (Hindi).

The process hasn't stopped, either. Today English is spoken in different forms and variations by about 350 million people across the world. That's more than one tenth of the world population for whom English is their first language and numbers are growing rapidly because English is the language of the Internet.

Meanwhile, back in Britain, about 7% of the population is bilingual because they, or their ancestors, moved to Britain from elsewhere. So words, from Caribbean and Indian languages, in particular, are still finding their way into English.

New words are invented to suit new situations, too. A 'nimby' is a 1980s word for someone who doesn't want new building near his or her home. It stood originally for 'Not In My Back Yard'. Computer vocabulary such as 'megabyte' and 'download' are fairly new arrivals too.

So – I hope that point is proved – the English language is colossal, sizeable, huge, gigantic, immense, gargantuan, substantial, massive, tremendous and vast – and we have lots of synonyms!

English is slippery and delicious. It doesn't always work quite as you expect it to. That's what makes it so exciting to work with. It's also what makes it tricky – so it's important to get to grips with as many of the finer points as you can. This book will help you to do so. Each chapter starts with two passages to read. I've selected works by writers whom I admire very much and I hope you will too. Some have been written for a long time. Others are 'hot off the press' and have been published in the same year as this book. Reading will help you to absorb ever more of those half-a-million words which are out there waiting eagerly for you. So do read as many as you can of the titles listed in the 'Have you read?' sections.

Write as much as you can, too. Writing is to English what running is to sport. It keeps your muscles working and your energy levels high. I am a professional writer as well as a teacher and I know that years of regular writing have done wonders for my command of English. Each chapter has some ideas for you to use as starting points for your own writing.

You also need to learn how to put words together and how to spell and punctuate precisely. Did you know that spelling wasn't fixed until the 18th century and that Shakespeare is said to have spelled his name in thirteen different ways? Don't feel too envious, though. Think how difficult reading must have been when you couldn't tell 'meet' from 'meat' or 'sight' from 'site' or 'lesson' from 'lessen'.

Have fun with it!

Chapter 1

Food, glorious food

Oliver Twist has no family. He lives, in the 1830s, in a workhouse. A workhouse was a building in which paupers (poor people) were kept, often very uncomfortably or even cruelly.

1   The room in which the boys were fed was a large stone hall with a copper[1] at one end. Out of this the master, dressed in an apron for the purpose, and assisted by one or two of the women, ladled the gruel[2] at mealtimes. Of this festive composition each boy had one small portion and no more – except on occasions of great public rejoicing when he had
5   two ounces and a quarter of bread besides.

     The bowls never needed washing. The boys polished them with their spoons till they shone. When they had performed this operation (which never took very long, the spoons being nearly as large as the bowls) they would sit eagerly staring at the copper as if they could have devoured the very bricks of which it was composed. They employed
10   themselves meanwhile in sucking their fingers most assiduously with the view of catching any stray splashes of gruel that might have landed there.

     Boys generally have excellent appetites. Oliver Twist and his companions had suffered the tortures of slow starvation for three months. At last they got so voracious and wild with hunger that one boy who was tall for his age hinted darkly to his companions that,
15   unless he got another basin of gruel each day, he was afraid he might happen to eat the boy who slept next to him. He had a wild, hungry eye and they believed him.

     A council was held. The boys drew lots to decide who should walk up to the master that evening and ask for more. The lot fell to Oliver Twist.

     The evening arrived and the boys took their places. The master in his cook's uniform
20   stationed himself at the copper. His pauper assistants ranged themselves behind him. The gruel was served out and a long grace was said over the meagre meal.

     The gruel disappeared. The boys whispered to each other and winked at Oliver, while his next neighbour nudged him. Child as he was, he was desperate with hunger and reckless with misery. He rose from the table, somewhat alarmed at his own temerity and
25   advancing to the master, basin and spoon in hand, said:

     'Please, Sir, I want some more.'

     The master was a fat, healthy man but he turned very pale. He gazed in stupefied astonishment at the small rebel for some seconds and then clung for support to the copper. The assistants were paralysed with wonder; the boys with fear.

30   'What?' said the master at length, in a faint voice.

'Please, Sir,' replied Oliver, 'I want some more.'

The master aimed a blow at Oliver's head with the ladle, pinioned him in his arms and shrieked aloud for Mr Bumble, the Beadle.

35   For a week after the commission of the impious and profane offence of asking for more, Oliver Twist remained a close prisoner in a dark and solitary room. It was nice cold weather and he was allowed to wash every morning under the pump in the stone yard in the presence of Mr Bumble, who prevented his catching cold by repeated applications of the cane. And every other day he was carried into the hall where the boys dined and was sociably beaten as a public warning and example.

(Adapted from *Oliver Twist* by Charles Dickens)

Notes:
[1] A large metal container for heating liquid; this one is built into a brick case
[2] Thin porridge

Exercise 1.1

Read the extract *Food, glorious food* and answer these questions as fully as you can:

1.   How long was it since the boys had eaten well?

2.   Explain why the bowls never needed washing (line 6).

3.   Why was Oliver the one who asked for more?

4.   Give another word for (a) assiduously (line 10), (b) stationed (line 20), (c) temerity (line 24) and (d) pinioned (line 32).

5. How was Oliver punished after he had asked for more?

6. Why does Dickens call one basin of gruel 'festive' in the first paragraph (line 3) when in the fifth paragraph he refers to it as a 'meagre meal'(line 21)?

Child obesity alert

Parents urged to tackle problem of overweight children

1   Schools and parents must take action to combat a health time bomb linked to childhood obesity. Speaking about the issue, Dr Brian Gaffney, Chief Executive of the Health Promotion Agency, said: 'We know from research that what children eat and drink when they are young can affect their health for many years to come. So, developing good
5   eating habits at an early age is crucial.'

    Research carried out by the Agency shows that a third of boys and a quarter of girls aged 12 carry excess weight. Research also shows that obesity can impact on a child's life on many levels. Obesity can present immediate and future health problems including high blood pressure, an increased risk of heart disease and diabetes. Overweight
10   children can also suffer from psychological problems such as depression or a lack of self-esteem and self-confidence.

    There are many ways to combat this growing problem of obesity, including providing children with a healthy, varied, balanced diet, rich in fruit and vegetables, both at school and at home, as well as increasing physical activity levels, both at school and outside
15   school, which will improve their overall health and well being.

(From Health Promotion Agency website 2004)

Exercise 1.2

Read the extract 'Child obesity alert' and answer these questions as fully as you can:

1. In a group of (a) 90 boys and (b) 100 girls, how many of each are likely to be too heavy?
2. What possible health problems could face overweight children once they have grown up?
3. What is the meaning of the word 'obesity' (line 2)?
4. How are obese children likely to feel about themselves now?
5. What can be done to make sure children don't have these problems?
6. Why is the situation described as a 'time bomb' (line 1)?
7. Who do you think the Health Promotion Agency hopes will read this notice?

Exercise 1.3

Your turn to write:

1. Imagine you are Oliver Twist. Write your diary for the day you asked for more and the days which followed. Use your imagination and add to the basic story. Invent as much detail as you like.

2. Write a story about a hungry child in a difficult situation. He or she might be in Britain today or at some point in the past or, perhaps, in some other country where there is hunger today.

3. Do you agree that too many children eat an unhealthy diet? Set out your views in a short article for parents to read, perhaps in a school magazine or newsletter.

4. Write a detailed description of the most memorable meal you have ever eaten. Include where you were and who you were with.

5. Write in any way you choose about food.

Grammar and punctuation

Full stops

Every sentence must end in a full stop. Sometimes the full stop is part of a question mark or an exclamation mark. You might see

.   ?   or   !

at the end of sentences. It is quite wrong to end a sentence in any other way – for example with a comma.

Use a question mark if your sentence asks a question such as:

> Does your dog like corn flakes?

Use an exclamation mark if your sentence says something unexpected or makes a surprised comment such as:

> Your dog likes corn flakes!

Use a full stop for all other sorts of sentence such as:

> I've never met a dog which likes corn flakes.

We shall learn more about question marks and exclamation marks later. In this chapter we concentrate on the full stop.

**A full stop chatting to a question mark
and an exclamation mark**

Starting a sentence

It is quite easy to tell when a new sentence begins because the first word of every sentence has to have a capital letter. Make sure that, when you write sentences, you make the difference between capital and small letters very clear.

Sometimes capital letters are called 'upper case' letters. Similarly small letters are sometimes known as 'lower case' letters. This was because printers used to store their individual letters in separate containers (cases) one above the other. The upper case contained the capital letters and the lower one the small letters. Old-fashioned typewriters copied this arrangement.

Capital / Upper case:

A B C D E F G H I J K L M N O P Q R S T U V W X Y Z

Small / Lower case:

a b c d e f g h i j k l m n o p q r s t u v w x y z

Exercise 1.4

Write out the sentences below with the capital letters and full stops in the right places. Each one consists of two sentences.

1. life in a Victorian workhouse was very harsh residents were often hungry
2. at times Oliver felt very lonely his mother had died when he was born
3. too many British children are obese experts think more exercise would help
4. vegetables are good for you too many burgers are not
5. Oliver asked the other boys watched
6. I don't like porridge my mother does

Exercise 1.5

Five of these are complete sentences. The other three are not. Write out the ones which are already sentences with a capital letter at the beginning and a full stop at the end. Ignore the others.

1. *Oliver Twist* and *Nicholas Nickelby*, books by Charles Dickens
2. Dickens wrote *Oliver Twist*
3. Some food can help to make you too fat
4. oranges are my favourite fruit
5. you should always eat your greens
6. spinach and broccoli
7. pasta is an Italian food
8. the Chinese restaurant near us

Now add words of your own to convert the three you have left over into correctly-punctuated sentences.

Exercise 1.6

1. Write out this story with capital letters and full stops in the right places:

   Emma has had a bad week on Monday she was late for school because of a traffic jam Tuesday was worse there was rice for lunch Emma hates rice on Wednesday she cut her finger on the bread knife at breakfast time

   things got worse as the week went on in the supermarket with her mother on Thursday, Emma dropped a dozen eggs as she was putting them in the trolley then, on Friday, she fell over the cat and sprained her ankle

   so she went to bed early on Friday evening she had a nightmare

2. If you get that finished quickly, write a few lines of your own in which everything goes right for Emma. Make sure every sentence ends with a full stop.

Nouns

A noun is the name given to a person, place or thing. There are three main types of noun: common, proper and abstract.

(a)   The following words are all **common** nouns:

gruel   spoons
man   pauper
children   fruit

A common noun

(b)   Names of people, for example Charles Dickens, Mr Bumble or Dr Brian Gaffney, are **proper** nouns. So are the names of towns such as Horsham or of rivers such as the Tyne or the Thames. Proper nouns **always** begin with a capital letter.

(c)   Finally, abstract nouns are nouns which name feelings, ideas or things which we talk and write about but which can't be touched:

diet   problems
obesity   hunger
improvement   misery

Exercise 1.7

A proper noun

Noun activities:

1.   Think of a fruit or vegetable for every letter of the alphabet. Have fun with this and try to think of some unusual ones: avocado, breadfruit, chard, damson. . .? These are ordinary, **common** nouns.

2.   Think of a boy's name, which is a **proper** noun, for every letter of the alphabet. Be as unusual as you can. Augustus, Bartholomew, Cuthbert . . . .? If you write them down, check that you have used a capital letter for each. Then repeat it with girls' names. You are working, remember, with proper nouns.

3.   Write down the word for every feeling you can think of, such as sadness, hunger, joy, excitement, thirst, tiredness . . . These are **abstract** nouns.

An abstract noun

Vocabulary and spelling

1. **Voracious** means hungry. It is related to the word 'devour' which means 'to swallow' or 'eat up greedily'. The following words also often mean 'hungry' although they can be used in slightly different senses:

    gluttonous   ravenous   ravening   craving   greedy   rapacious

Look up the exact meaning of these words in a dictionary and experiment with them in sentences of your own.

2. **Crucial** means 'central'. It comes from the Latin word for 'cross' (*crux, crucis*). If something is crucial it is as if it is at the centre of a cross and therefore very important.

    If you say something is 'the **crux** of the matter' you mean it is the centre point of the issue.

    Jesus was **crucified** or attached to a cross to die.

    Cruciform or **cruciate** means 'shaped like a cross'.

    A **cruciverbalist** is someone who loves crosswords.

Use these words in sentences of your own.

3. Look at the spelling of **meagre**. It ends with 're.' So do:

    theatre   centre   acre   ochre   sabre

Do not muddle these with similar sounding words which end in 'er' and do not be confused if you see these words spelt otherwise. Americans have different spelling rules so you have to be on your guard if you are using British English; and beware the spellcheck on your computer – it is often set to American spellings!

4. **Immediate** has a double 'm'. So do:

command	common	commit	grammar
glimmer	hammer	commence	hammock
immense	recommend	accommodate	commerce
clammy	commission	ammonia	commotion

Learn the spellings of these words by writing them down several times. Look up the meanings of any that you do not know.

Speaking and listening

1. Make a class play out of the incident in *Oliver Twist* when Oliver asks for more. Perhaps you could perform it to the rest of the school in assembly.

2. Work with a partner. Choose a fruit or vegetable. Prepare a talk for the rest of the class about it. Mention all the delicious ways there are of eating it, or – if you prefer – talk about why you dislike whatever it is you have chosen to talk about.

3. Work with someone in the class you don't know very well. Find out what he or she likes to eat. Take it in turns to do this. Then join with another pair. Tell the other pair about your partner's eating preferences and dislikes.

4. Get a copy of *Oliver Twist* – or any other book by Charles Dickens. Find a short passage that appeals to you and practise reading it aloud. Then hear each other's readings in small groups.

Have you read?

All these books are about children who are hungry, poor or who find themselves in difficult situations:

Oliver Twist by Charles Dickens (Ladybird Classics 2003; or Penguin Popular Classics 1994)
A Christmas Carol by Charles Dickens (Ladybird Classics 1994; or Wordsworth Children's
    Classics 1993)
Black Harvest by Ann Pilling (Collins Modern Classics 1999)
Rice Without Rain by Min Fong Ho (Heinemann New Windmills 1989)
Up on Cloud Nine by Anne Fine (Corgi Children's Paperback 2003)
The Breadwinner by Deborah Ellis (OUP 2004)
The Family From One End Street by Eve Garnett (Puffin Modern Classics 2004)
The Ghost Behind the Wall by Melvyn Burgess (Puffin 2002)

And if you've done all that

● Find out about the life of Charles Dickens through encyclopaedias and the Internet. Prepare a short talk about him for the rest of the class.

● Make a class recipe leaflet or booklet by collecting from each pupil in your class a favourite family recipe. If you can use a computer to make it look professional, you might be able to sell it to parents and friends in aid of one of the charities working with hungry children, such as Save the Children (www.savethechildren.org.uk) or Oxfam (www.oxfam.org.uk).

● Read *Oliver Twist*. Then see – or see again – the 1968 film of Lionel Bart's musical *Oliver!* If your school does not have a video or DVD of it, you will be able to borrow it from almost any library. In which ways are the stories different? Why do you think the film makers made these changes?

Chapter 2

Mermaids

Roger and Polly are rowing with their mysterious French friend Melusine on a canal at La Venise Verte in the Vendée area of France.

1   'We can't change places here. I'll pull into the bank.' Roger laid hold of the oars and prepared to turn.

'It's okay. I'll just –'

Polly stood up just as he started to turn toward the bank – hit her head on the half-fallen
5   tree – and fell straight out of the boat.

The clonk of her head hitting the wood, the leap of the boat as she left it and the loud splash caused Roger to drop the oars and spin round. She hadn't screamed. She vanished into the scummy water and it closed over her head without sound.

'Polly! Polly!' he bellowed, more in fury than in fright at first. Then, when nothing
10   happened, his voice rose to a squeak of terror. '*Polly*!'

Silence. Roger's wits completely deserted him. He half stood, half crouched there in the rocking boat, expecting her head to break the surface, expecting – expecting it not to have happened.

But it had. She was gone.

15   Suddenly the boat leapt again. Instinctively he clutched the gunwales to steady himself, and looked toward the stern.

Melusine was gone.

He saw only the swirl in the green water beside where she had been seated. And something – a blackish undulating line – her pigtail? – wiggled, swished audibly
20   through the turbulence and disappeared.

Desperately he prepared to jump in. But something stopped him. There was some underwater upheaval occurring just below the boat that upset his balance and made him crouch down again instinctively. Something big was threshing about down there.

25 Roger was paralysed with shock, with fear. He could think of only one thing, sitting there clinging to the oarlocks with white knuckles.

A crocodile . . .impossible! And yet . . .

Then suddenly there was a bubbling burst of sound. Polly's head had shot out of the water as if propelled from below. Her face was ghastly, deathly white under streaks of glistening mud, her hair plastered to her skull.

30 As Roger reached out and grabbed any bit of her he could get hold of he felt her body being shoved higher by something unseen in the depths.

Polly lay in the bottom of the boat, streams of water pouring from her hair, her clothes. He threw himself on to her back with all his strength and more water gushed out of her mouth and nose. She gave a retching cough and then he heard a great noisy gasp of air rush into
35 her lungs. It was the most marvellous relieving sound he had ever heard in his life.

Melusine . . . !

He looked round wildly. And at once he saw her! He felt all the blood leave his face.

She was crouching in the boat just behind him. Her face was pale, exhausted even, but composed. After drying Polly a little, she took off her life jacket and after it the jacket
40 she was wearing. She spread this lengthways over Polly to warm her.

Roger crouched there, unable to move. His eyes were riveted to the jacket.

It was perfectly dry.

Roger reached out and touched the leg of Melusine's trousers.

They were dry. *She was dry all over*. Her pigtail, that he had distinctly seen vanishing
45 into the canal, was dry. She had not a drop of water on her.

(Slightly abridged from *Melusine* by Lynne Reid Banks)

Exercise 2.1

Read the extract *Mermaids* and answer these questions as fully as you can:

1. Explain how Polly comes to fall out of the boat.
2. Give another word for (a) turbulence (line 20), (b) propelled (line 28) and (c) riveted (line 41).
3. Why does Roger not jump into the water to rescue Polly?
4. What indications are there in this passage that Melusine is not quite what she seems?
5. List six words from the passage which suggest Roger's fear.
6. Why do you think Lynne Reid Banks often uses very short sentences and paragraphs here?

A mermaid-like sea mammal

1   The dugong, or sea cow, lives in the south-west Pacific and the Indian Ocean.

A sea cow's life is not a demanding one. They trundle through the underwater meadows propelled entirely by the slow downward sweep of their huge tail. Since they live on plants, and plants need light in order to grow, they have no reason to swim to any depth.

5   They are so big that few other swimmers can attack them and sharks only seldom venture into these shallow waters.

Dugongs live off the tropical coasts of Australia in scattered herds and tend to patrol the same paths like a herd of domestic terrestrial cows.

When a young sea cow is born it suckles milk from a nipple in its mother's armpit.

10   Since it and its mother are, of course, air-breathing the mothers may at this time rear out of the water to allow their drinking young to breathe. It is this, some say, that gave rise to legends of the mermaid.

(Adapted from *The Life of Mammals* by David Attenborough)

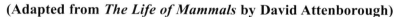

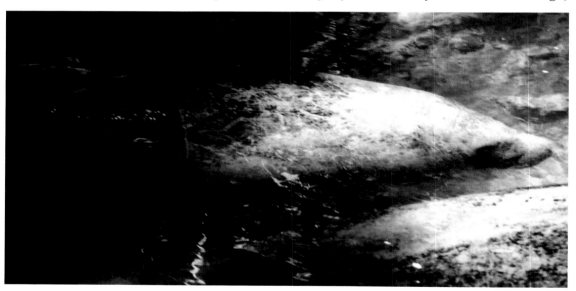

Exercise 2.2

Read the extract *A mermaid-like sea mammal* and answer these questions as fully as you can:

1.   In what three ways is the dugong's life 'not a demanding one'?

2.   Where are sea cows found? Be as accurate as you can.

3.   Which is the only animal which might attack a dugong?

4.   Why is the sea cow associated with mermaids?

5.   Which two words suggest that David Attenborough does not fully believe that the sea cow could be mistaken for a mermaid?

Exercise 2.3

Your turn to write:

1.   Write a story about a mermaid (or merman).

2.   Describe a sea mammal in careful detail. You might choose a seal, dolphin, whale or sea lion, for example. Include its appearance, habits, where it lives, its food, breeding and so on. Use reference books to find the information and your own knowledge if you have seen the creature yourself or watched a TV programme about it.

3.   Read one of the books listed in 'Have you Read?' on page 19. Write a review of it.

4.   Write about water in any way you choose.

5.   Imagine you are Roger in the extract from *Melusine*. Write a letter or an email to a friend at home in England describing what happened at the canal. Invent as much extra detail of your own as you like.

Grammar and punctuation

The question mark

The question mark is very easy. Whenever the writer of a character in a story asks a question, it is followed by a question mark instead of a full stop. Most questions ask how? who? what? where? when? or why?

For example:

> When did you read a book by Lynne Reid Banks?
> Why doesn't David Attenborough believe in mermaids?
> 'Was it Melusine's pigtail?' wondered Roger.

A question mark

Exercise 2.4

Question mark activities:

Some of these sentences are, or include, questions. Others are not. Write out the ones which need question marks. (You should have five.)

(a)   Why wasn't Melusine wet
(b)   Melusine was dry
(c)   Fortunately Polly did not drown
(d)   What do dugongs eat
(e)   Does the dugong have another name
(f)   How many books has David Attenborough written
(g)   In 2002 he wrote *Life on Air*
(h)   Roger said 'I simply can't believe it'
(i)   'Who got me out of the canal' asked Polly

Tone of voice

In speech, British speakers of English usually lift the pitch of their voices (like singing a higher note) at the end of questions. It is a sort of spoken question mark.

Australian speakers of English do this with almost every sentence. Because we are so used to hearing Australian speech on TV, some British speakers of English (particularly young people) are beginning to do this too. It has the rather funny (to British ears) effect of making everything sound like a question.

More usually we drop the pitch of our voices (lower note) at the end of a statement – a spoken full stop. Experiment with saying:

'Sea cows are mammals' and **'Sea cows are mammals . . . ?'**

Say it first as a firm statement. Listen to where your voice goes. Now say it as a question and as if you are tentative or not sure of the answer. Your voice will have gone up.

Exercise 2.5

Make as many words of four letters and more as you can out of:

QUESTION MARK

Verbs

Verbs are the most important words in a language. They are 'action words' or 'being words'. They tell us what nouns are 'doing' or what they 'are'. Verbs are the glue which holds sentences together. If a group of words has no verb then it isn't really a sentence.

These are verbs:

bellowed	clutched
swished	wiggled
prepared	shoved
grabbed	gushed
trundle	suckles

Verbs often end in 's' or 'ed' depending on who is performing the action and when. They often consist of two or more words such as:

will go	was going
would have gone	will have gone

These words are used to change the **tense** of the verb, in other words to say **when** the action of the verb occurs (past, present or future). Good writers always choose strong colourful verbs.

Verbs are the glue which holds sentences together

Exercise 2.6

Put verbs of your own in the gaps in the following sentences:

1.   Water —— from the roof.

2.   Roger —— himself free.

3.   We —— France.

4.   My mother —— to —— and —— on holiday.

5.   Dugongs —— in the sea.

6.   David Attenborough often —— on television.

7.   Tomorrow I shall ——.

Exercise 2.7

Write out the following passage and underline the verbs. The first three have been done for you.

It <u>was</u> evening. Polly <u>had been seen</u> by a local doctor who <u>had wanted</u> to take her to hospital in Niort, the nearest large town thirty miles away, but in the end he had agreed that her mother could nurse her at home. He'd bandaged the bump on her head and said that she'd had a very narrow escape from drowning. When he said this, he scowled at her parents in a way that made them both hang their heads like guilty children.

Vocabulary and spelling

1.   **Audibly** means something is said or done so that it can be heard. It comes from the Latin verb *audio* = 'I hear'.

An **audience** was originally a group of people who listen to words or music. The word is now used more loosely to include people who watch something or even read it.

Audio-visual equipment is something like a DVD player which allows the user to hear as well as see.

The nerve which goes to the brain from the back of the ear is the **auditory** nerve.

An **auditorium** is the space in a theatre where the **audience** sits.

Audiology is the scientific study of hearing.

2.   **Terrestrial** means 'of the earth' (rather than of the sea or the air).

It comes from the Latin word *terra* which means earth or land.

Angleterre, as the French call England, means 'land of the Angles' (remember your Anglo-Saxons?).

Your **territory** is the land you are familiar with, own or have a right to.

Traditional reddish garden flower pots are made of **terra cotta** (baked earth).

An **extra-terrestrial** being comes from another world (particularly in films and stories).

3. Check that you know these ten spellings. All the words come from the two passages at the beginning of this chapter.

straight   deserted   instinctively   something   disappeared

desperately   relieving   exhausted   domestic   breathing

4. **They're, their, there**

They're means **they are**. The apostrophe marks the place of the missing letter. So 'They're hungry' means 'They are hungry' and 'They're arguing' means 'They are arguing'.

Their is a possessive pronoun (see below). It means 'belonging to them'. Melusine was the friend belonging to Roger and Polly so she was **their** friend. Dugongs find the food which belongs to them in shallow waters. They find **their** food.

If you mean anything other than 'they are' or 'belonging to them', use **there**.

Words such as these which **sound** the same but which have different spellings and meanings are called **homophones**.

Exercise 2.8

Write **they're**, **their** or **there** in the spaces in these sentences:

1. Dogs wag —— tails when —— happy.
2. Roger will moor the boat over ——
3. —— are some sea cows suckling —— young.
4. Polly and Melusine were both in the water so Roger, —— companion, was frightened.
5. Some mammals live —— lives in water.
6. The trees over —— will shed —— leaves soon because —— not evergreen.

Speaking and listening

1. Work with a partner. One of you pretends to believe in mermaids, the other does not. Rehearse your argument until it's like a little play. Then perform it to the rest of the class.
2. Work in a group. Pretend you're making a television advertisement for a trip to Australia to see the sea cows. You have to find ways of making it sound really attractive so that anyone seeing the advertisement will want to pay to go on the trip.
3. Work in a group of three. Take the parts of Roger, Polly and Melusine. Act out what happened in the boat. Use your own words and add extra details of your own.
4. Read one of the books on the list below. Then tell the rest of the class what you liked or disliked about it. If you enjoyed it, work out what you can say to persuade others to read it.
5. Describe to a partner in as much detail as you can your earliest memory of going in, or on, some kind of boat.

Have you read?

Most of these books are about children in boats or about mermaids:

Melusine by Lynne Reid Banks (HarperTrophy 1997)
The Life of Mammals by David Attenborough (BBC books 2002)
The Little Mermaid retold by Andrew Matthews (Orchard Fairy Tales 2001)
The Dolphin Crossing by Jill Paton Walsh (Penguin Modern Classics 1995)
Black Ivory by Norman Collins (Harper Collins)
In Deep Water by Michelle Magorian (Puffin 1994)
The Great Elephant Chase by Gillian Cross (OUP 2004)
Huckleberry Finn by Mark Twain (Puffin Classics 1995)
Swallows and Amazons by Arthur Ransome (Red Fox 2001)

And if you've done all that

- Research the legend of Melusine via the Internet or in an encyclopaedia. The German composer Felix Mendelssohn (1809-1847) wrote a piece of music called *The Fair Melusine*. Get it and listen to it. Your school music department may be able to help you find it or you could consult BBC Radio 3 which specialises in classical music (www.bbc.co.uk/radio3/). Decide how well you think the music fits the legend.

- Read two of the books on the list above and compare them in a written review. Say how they are different and what they have in common. Which did you prefer and why?

A note on possessive pronouns

There is lively debate and some confusion among some teachers and other adults, as to whether 'my', 'your', 'his', 'her', 'its' and 'their' should be classed as possessive pronouns or possessive adjectives. For more on this, see Chapter 9.

Chapter 3

The Elephant's Child

1   Once, a very long time ago, the elephant had no trunk. All he had was a blackish, bulgy nose as big as a boot. He could wriggle it about from side to side but he couldn't pick things up with it.

    Then a new elephant – an elephant's child – was born in Africa. He was full of 'satiable
5   curtiosity' which means he asked a lot of questions, although he was always very polite.

    He asked his tall aunt the Ostrich why her tail feathers grew just so. He asked his tall uncle the Giraffe what made his skin spotty. He asked his broad aunt the Hippopotamus why her eyes were red and he asked his hairy uncle the Baboon why melons tasted just so. They all told him off and shouted at him crossly, but he went on asking questions
10   about everything he saw, heard, felt, smelt or touched because he was still full of 'satiable curtiosity'.

    One fine morning this 'satiable elephant's child' asked a fine new question, most politely: 'What does the crocodile have for dinner?'

    His aunts and uncles all answered 'Hush!' in a loud and dreadful tone. They all looked
15   very angry with him. Suddenly the elephant's child saw the kolokolo bird perched on a thorn bush.

    'Everyone is cross with me because of my "satiable curtiosity,"' he told the kolokolo bird, 'but I still want to know what the crocodile has for dinner.'

    The kolokolo bird replied with a mournful cry, 'Go to the banks of the great, grey-green,
20   greasy Limpopo River all set about with fever trees and find out.'

    So, next morning the elephant's child assembled a hundred pounds of bananas (the short, red kind), a hundred pounds of sugar cane (the long, purple kind) and seventeen melons (the green, crinkly kind). He said goodbye to his grumpy family. Then he set off on a long journey. As he went, he looked about him, he munched melons, he ate
25   bananas and he crunched sugar cane. He threw down the rind, skins and leaves because, remember, he had no trunk with which to pick up his litter.

    At last he came to the banks of the great, grey-green, greasy Limpopo River all set about with fever trees, just as the kolokolo bird had said. Now, of course, until that very week and day and hour, the elephant's child had never seen a crocodile. It was all his
30   'satiable curtiosity'.

    The first thing the elephant's child found at the great, grey-green, greasy Limpopo River all set about with fever trees was a bi-coloured python rock snake. It was curled round a

rock and had a scalesome, flailsome tail. ''Scuse me,' said the elephant's child, 'but have you seen a crocodile in these provocative parts, and if you have, could you tell me
35   what he has for dinner?'

Like the elephant's child's aunts and uncles back home, the bi-coloured python rock snake crossly refused to answer. So the elephant's child walked along the bank of the great, grey-green, greasy Limpopo River scattering melon rinds he couldn't pick up – until he trod on what he thought was a log. But really it was a crocodile! The crocodile
40   winked cunningly and shed a few crocodile tears.

''Scuse me,' said the elephant's child most politely, 'but do you happen to have seen a crocodile in these provocative parts? And, if you have, could you tell me what he has for dinner, please?' The crocodile winked the other eye and lifted his tail out of the mud.

'Come hither little one,' said the crocodile. 'Why do you ask such things?'

45   'My tall aunt the Ostrich, my tall uncle the Giraffe, my broad aunt the Hippopotamus, my hairy uncle the Baboon and the bi-coloured python rock snake all got furious with me when I asked but I still want to know,' said the elephant's child.

'Come hither little one,' said the crocodile, 'for I am the crocodile. Come hither and I'll whisper.' Then the elephant's child put his head down close to the crocodile's musky,
50   tusky mouth and the crocodile caught him by his little nose which, until that moment, had been no bigger than a boot, although much more useful.

'I think,' said the crocodile, through his teeth, 'that today I will begin with this elephant's child.'

The elephant's child was frightened and tried to back away, shouting through his nose:
55   'Led go! You're hurdig me!'

Then the bi-coloured python rock snake scuffled down the bank and said: 'My young friend, tug as hard as ever you can or that crocodile will quickly jerk you into yonder limpid stream.' (This is the way bi-coloured python rock snakes always talk.)

60 So the elephant's child sat back on his little haunches and pulled and pulled and pulled until his nose began to stretch. The crocodile flailed about in the water making it all creamy with great sweeps of his tail. He too pulled and pulled and pulled.

The elephant's child's nose grew longer and longer. He stretched all four of his little legs and pulled and pulled and pulled. The crocodile threshed his tail like an oar as he pulled and pulled and pulled. By now the elephant's child's nose was hurting a lot and
65 was nearly five feet long. 'This is too butch for me,' he said through his long nose.

Then the bi-coloured python rock snake came down the bank and knotted his scalesome, flailsome tail tightly round the elephant's child's hind legs. He pulled and the elephant's child pulled and the crocodile pulled but the bi-coloured python rock snake pulled the hardest. At last the crocodile let go of the elephant's child with a plop you could hear all up
70 and down the Limpopo (still great, grey-green, greasy and all set about with fever trees).

The elephant's child carefully put wet banana leaves on his sore nose and sat on the bank of the great, grey-green, greasy Limpopo river for three days waiting for his stretched nose to shrink. But the bi-coloured python rock snake told him it wouldn't grow any shorter and it didn't. The crocodile had pulled it into a really-truly trunk, the
75 same as all elephants have today.

After a while a fly came and stung him on the shoulder. Before he knew what he was doing the elephant's child had lifted up his trunk and hit that fly dead with the end of it.

''Vantage number one!' said the bi-coloured python rock snake. 'You couldn't have done that with a mere-smear nose. Try and eat a little now.'

80 Before he could think what he was doing the elephant's child had put out his trunk, plucked a large bundle of grass, dusted it clean against his fore legs and stuffed it into his own mouth.

''Vantage number two!' said the bi-coloured python rock snake. 'You couldn't have done that with a mere-smear nose. Don't you think the sun is awfully hot here?'

85 'It is,' said the elephant's child and, before he had thought about it, he had schlooped up a schloop of mud from the banks of the great, grey-green, greasy Limpopo River and slapped it on his head where it made a cool schloopy-sloshy mud-cap all trickly behind his ears.

''Vantage number three!' said the bi-coloured python rock snake. 'You couldn't have
90 done that with a mere-smear nose.'

With that the elephant's child thanked the bi-coloured python rock snake, said goodbye and set off on the long journey home across Africa to his family. As he went he frisked and whisked his new trunk.

When he wanted grass he could pick it up from the ground without bending. When flies
95 bit him he used his trunk to break off a branch of a tree to use as a fly-swat. When he felt hot in the African sun his trunk made him a slushy-squashy mud-cap.

If he felt lonely he sang to himself through his trunk and made a trumpeting noise louder than several brass bands. As he went along he picked up the melon rinds, banana skins and sugar-cane leaves he had dropped on his way there, for he was a tidy
100   pachyderm.

At last he reached home. There, several members of his family spoke to him: his brothers, his hairy uncle the Baboon, his tall aunt the Ostrich, his tall uncle the Giraffe and his broad aunt the Hippopotamus. 'Oh bananas! What have you done to your nose?' asked one of his brothers.

105   'I got a new one from the crocodile on the banks of the great, grey-green, greasy Limpopo River,' explained the elephant's child. 'I asked him what he had for dinner and he gave me this to keep.'

'It looks very ugly,' said his hairy uncle the Baboon, cross as usual.

'It does, but it's useful,' replied the elephant's child, using his trunk to pick up his hairy
110   uncle the Baboon and throw him into a wasps' nest.

Then that bad elephant's child took his revenge on all his relations who had been so bad-tempered with him in the past. This is what he did: he pulled out his tall Ostrich aunt's tail feathers. He caught his tall uncle the Giraffe by the hind-legs and dragged him through a thorn bush and he shouted at his broad aunt the Hippopotamus and blew
115   bubbles into her ear when she was sleeping in the water after meals. But he never let anyone touch the kolokolo bird.

At last things grew so exciting that all his family went off one by one in a hurry to the banks of the great, grey-green, greasy Limpopo River all set about with fever trees, to borrow new noses from the crocodile. That is why all the elephants you will ever see,
120   beside all those that you won't, have trunks like that of the 'satiably curtious' elephant's child.

(Adapted from *Just So Stories* by Rudyard Kipling)

Exercise 3.1

Read the extract *The Elephant's Child* and answer these questions as fully as you can:

1.   Why did the elephant's child leave his family?

2.   Apart from the elephant's child, which animal do you find the most interesting in this story? Explain your choice.

3.   Give another word for (a) assembled (line 21), (b) hither (line 44) and (c) threshed (line 63).

4.   Explain why the elephant's child is pleased with his new trunk.

5.   When the elephant's child says 'satiable curtiosity' (e.g. in line 11) and 'provocative' (e.g. in line 34) he is making mistakes in his English because he is still very young. Can you work out what he really means?

Elephants in zoos

1   FROM DR ROB ATKINSON

Sir,

The RSPCA[1] wants zoos to stop keeping elephants because of animal welfare concerns. It has nothing to do with politics, as suggested by Richard Morrison (T2, September 29).
5   RSPCA-commissioned scientific research shows that elephants in European zoos live nowhere near the 60-65 years they can reach in the wild. They die young, having suffered from deficient enclosures, poor diet, illness, inappropriate social grouping, and even rough treatment by their handlers. Zoo-breeding programmes also have an abysmal record – about a third of zoo-born babies die within a year, many of which are stillborn,
10   or rejected or even killed by their mothers.

Because they fail to keep flourishing captive populations, zoos have to import elephants from their native lands. Yet they claim to keep elephants for conservation reasons. The costs of housing elephants properly in European zoos are prohibitive, and that money would be better spent protecting elephants in the wild.

15   Yours sincerely,
ROB ATKINSON
(Head, Wildlife Department),
RSPCA,
Southwater,
20   Horsham, West Sussex RH13 9RS
October 3rd

(Published in *The Times* on Monday 6th October 2003)

Note:
[1] RSPCA stands for Royal Society for Prevention of Cruelty to Animals

Exercise 3.2

Read the letter about elephants in zoos and then answer these questions as fully as you can:

1. What is Rob Atkinson's job?
2. Where is the RSPCA's head office?
3. Why does Mr Atkinson think it is cruel to keep elephants in zoos?
4. Why is it expensive to keep elephants in zoos?
5. What would Mr Atkinson prefer the money to be spent on?
6. What has made Mr Atkinson write this letter to *The Times* newspaper?
7. Give another word for (a) deficient (line 7), (b) abysmal (line 8) and (c) prohibitive (line 13).

Exercise 3.3

Your turn to write:

1. Write your own *Just So* story of how the dog got its bark, how the tiger got its stripes, how the bird got its wings or how the kangaroo got its pocket.
2. Imagine you are an elephant and tell the story of something which has happened to you. You could set your story in Africa or India or in a zoo.
3. What do you think about elephants in zoos? Write a letter to *The Times* either agreeing or disagreeing with Mr Atkinson.
4. Did you enjoy *The Elephant's Child*? Write your views. Say what you liked and disliked about it.
5. Imagine that you are trying to communicate with someone who has never seen, heard, touched or smelled an elephant. He or she has never even seen a picture in a book or on television. Describe an elephant for him or her in as much detail and as accurately as you can. Don't forget to mention its appearance, size, colour, shape, habits, the sounds it makes and how it smells.

Grammar and punctuation

Commas for lists

Commas are used to separate items in a list within a sentence. You do not need a comma between the last two items when you use 'and' or 'or'.

For example:

> . . . everything he saw, heard, felt, smelt or touched . . .
>
> . . . he looked about him, he munched melons, he ate bananas and he crunched sugar-cane . . .
>
> . . . melon rinds, banana skins and sugar-cane leaves . . .
>
> . . . great, grey-green, greasy Limpopo River. . .

A comma in a list

Commas acting as brackets

Commas are also used to fence off words or phrases which are not essential to the main meaning of the sentence.

For example:

> He threw down the rind, skins and leaves because, remember, he had no trunk with which to pick up his litter. (remember)

> There, several members of his family spoke to him. (there)

A comma acting as brackets

Exercise 3.4

Read these sentences. Put the commas into the lists they contain:

1. Elephants like to eat melons bananas leaves grasses and other plants.

2. The elephant's nose was tugged yanked dragged heaved and stretched by the crocodile.

3. Near the river bank lay a clever talkative helpful and knowledgeable python.

4. Should elephants lions tigers gorillas and bears be kept in zoos?

5. You could ask your mother father sister brother aunt or uncle what they think.

Exercise 3.5

Read these sentences. Add words in the spaces fenced off by commas. You can use your own words or choose from the list below:

1. The elephant's child, ... , was insatiably curious.

2. His relations, ... , refused to answer questions patiently.

3. ..., on the banks of the Limpopo, a frantic struggle took place.

4. Listen, ..., and I'll tell you a story.

5. If you want advice, ..., ask a rock-snake.

(remember   of course   however   nearby   there   you see   my child)

And if you get that finished quickly, write six sentences of your own which need commas, either for separating items in the list or for fencing off words. The correct term for 'fencing off' words is **parenthesis**.

Adjectives

Adjectives tell us more about nouns. We say that they qualify (or modify) nouns.

> great
> grey-green
> greasy
> tall
> useful
> slushy-squashy
> rough
> scientific

An adjective introducing himself to a noun

So, for example, Rudyard Kipling qualifies Limpopo (a proper noun) by telling us that it's great, grey-green and greasy; Mr Atkinson (on p. 24) writes not just about research (an abstract noun) but about scientific research.

Exercise 3.6

Adjective activities:

1. Play the 'Gladys's Cat' game in groups of four. The first player says, for example, 'Gladys's cat is an adventurous cat'. The second says something like 'Gladys's cat is an admirable cat,' and you take turns until everyone has said the sentence with an original adjective starting with 'a'. Then you move onto 'b': 'Gladys's cat is a bouncy cat' and so on. No repeats are allowed and you must use the whole sentence every time. The big challenge comes when you're the fourth person to get 'x'!

2. Write a poem about an animal, using strings of adjectives starting with the same letter, as Kipling uses 'great, grey-green, greasy'. You could also try to make some of them rhyme, for example 'musky tusky'.

3. Adjectives are often formed from nouns. Fill in the adjectives on this list. The first two have been done for you:

Noun	Adjective
elephant	elephantine
bulge	bulgy
obedience	...
thickness	...
success	...
curiosity	...
naughtiness	...
circle	...
picture	...

Vocabulary and spelling

1. **Elephantine** is, of course, an adjective meaning elephant-like. Find out the meanings of these adjectives: feline, aquiline, porcine, vulpine.

2. A **pachyderm** is a large animal with a thick skin such as a rhinoceros, hippopotamus or elephant. *Pakhus* is the Ancient Greek word for 'thick' and *derma* means 'skin'.

    So whenever you see 'derm' or 'derma' in a word it has probably got something to do with skin:

    > **Dermatitis** is a skin disease.
    > A **dermatologist** is a doctor specialising in skin problems.
    > If you describe something as **dermatoid** you mean it looks like skin.

3. A **native** is a person or an animal who was born in a certain place, so an elephant's native land is Africa or India. If you are a native of Surrey it means that you were born there. To the Romans, who spoke and wrote Latin, the word *natus* meant 'born' and that's where this word comes from. Look out for connections in other words:

    > A **nativity** play is about Jesus's birth.
    > If something is **natural** to you it means you were born with the ability to do it.
    > Your **nature** is the character you were born with.

    Use these words in some sentences of your own.

4. Look at the spelling of **stretch**. It's quite an unusual word because it has seven letters but only one vowel. It includes 'str' and ' tch'. Can you spell these words?

strength	batch
string	fetch
strong	latch
strung	hutch
stroll	pitch
struck	notch

    Take care, while you are about it, with 'yacht', which looks as if it is in the same spelling family but is not.

    Learn the spellings of all these words with a friend and then test each other.

Speaking and listening

1. Work in pairs. Practise reading *The Elephant's Child* aloud together. Discuss how you're going to split it up. Then perform your reading to the rest of the class.

2. Find an animal poem. Learn it by heart. Organise a class 'poetry festival' where you take turns to say your poems.

3. Work with a partner. Invent a two-person play in which one of you believes that animals should be kept in zoos and the other thinks that all zoos should be closed. Work out roughly what you will say to each other. Then perform what you've practised to another pair in the class. The proper name for this work is *rôle play*.

Have you read?

The following books are all about animals:

Just So Stories by Rudyard Kipling (Penguin Classics 1994)
The Jungle Book by Rudyard Kipling (Puffin 1994) – This contains some good animal stories such as *Rikki-Tikki-Tavi* as well as the two Mowgli stories immortalised by Walt Disney.
The Sheep-pig by Dick King Smith (Puffin 1999)
Charlotte's Web by EB White (Puffin 1963)
How the Whale Became by Ted Hughes (Faber and Faber 1989)
The Road to Somewhere by Helen Armstrong (Orion 2001)
The Road to the River by Helen Armstrong (Orion 2002)
Watership Down by Richard Adams (Puffin 1973)
Tarka the Otter by Henry Williamson (Puffin 1995)
Black Beauty by Anna Sewell (Penguin Classics 1995)

And if you've done all that

*   Look up the RSPCA and World Wildlife Fund in an encyclopaedia or on the Internet (www.rspca.org.uk; www.wwf-uk.org). Prepare a short talk about their work for the rest of the class.

*   Read one of the last three recommended books on the reading list (they are longer than the others on the list). Tell the rest of the class about the book and what you liked or disliked about it.

*   How many different ways can you think of in which human beings make use of animals? Write a list. Work out which of these you think is fair and right and which you think is not, and why. For example, you might, perhaps approve of a guide dog working for a blind person but be unhappy about bull fighting. Write your views down or make them into a talk for part or all of your class.

Chapter 4

The Second World War (1939-45)

Chas McGill collects war souvenirs. It is the winter of 1940/1. Tyneside, where Chas lives, is being relentlessly bombed by the Germans.

1   The wood was bleak and ugly too. Grown-ups dumped rubbish round the outside, and kids climbed and broke the trees. But nobody went into the middle. Some said it was haunted but Chas had never found anything there but a feeling of cold misery, which wasn't exciting like a headless horseman. Still, it was an oddly discouraging sort of place.

5   Every year the briars grew thicker. Even Chas knew only one way through them. He took it now, wriggling under the arches of briar as thick as your finger, interlaced like barbed wire. He picked himself up quickly because the grass was soaking. The sky seemed greyer through the bare branches and he felt fed up. Still, since he was here he might as well search for souvenirs.

10 He sniffed. There was a funny, foreign smell in the wood . . . like petrol and fireworks. Funny – it wasn't Guy Fawkes yet. Some kids must have been messing about. As he pressed on, the smell grew stronger. There must be an awful lot of petrol.

Something was blocking out the light through the branches. A new building; a secret army base; a new anti-aircraft gun? He couldn't quite see except that it was black.

15 And then he saw, quite clearly at the top, a swastika[1], black – outlined in white. He didn't know whether to run towards it or away. So he stayed stock-still, listening. Not a sound. He moved forward again.

He burst into the clearing. It was the tail of the German aircraft which had crashed on the laundry. At least, most of it had crashed on the laundry. The tail, breaking off in the
20 air, had spun to earth like a sycamore seed. He'd read of that happening in books. He could also tell from books that this had been a *Heinkel He111*[2].

Chas sighed. If he reported it, they'd just come and take it away for scrap. Like when he'd taken that shiny new incendiary-bomb rack to the Warden's post . . . they'd not even said thank you.

25 Chas gulped. The machine gun was still there, hanging from the turret, shiny and black.

He reached up and tugged at the round gun barrel. Then he grabbed it, put his plimsolls against the curving side of the plane and went up like a monkey. He peered over the edge of the cockpit.

The gunner was sitting there watching him. One hand, in a soft fur mitt, was stretched

30   up as if to retrieve the gun. The other lay in his overalled lap. He wore the black leather flying helmet of the Luftwaffe[3] and goggles. His right eye, pale grey, watched through the goggle glass tolerantly and a little sadly. He looked a nice man, young.

The glass of the other goggle was gone. Its rim was thick with sticky red. Inside was a seething mass of black flies, which rose and buzzed angrily at Chas's arrival, then sank
35   back into the goggle again.

For a terrible moment, Chas thought the Nazi was alive, that the mitted hand would reach out and grab him. Then, even worse, he knew he was dead.

(Adapted from *The Machine Gunners* by Robert Westall)

Notes:
[1] A squared-off cross used by Nazi Germany as a logo or symbol
[2] A German bomber
[3] The German air force

Exercise 4.1

Read the extract from *The Machine Gunners* and answer these questions as fully as you can:

1.   How does Robert Westall make the wood seem sinister even before Chas finds the aircraft tail?

2.   What is the first sign that there is something unusual to be found in the wood?

3.   What does Chas mainly want from the aircraft?

4.   Why does Westall tell us that the German gunner was watching Chas when later he tells us that the man was dead?

5.   Where was the rest of the aircraft?

6.   Give another word for (a) interlaced (line 6), (b) peered (line 27) and (c) retrieve (line 30).

Utility clothing

A group of people in the Milton Keynes area of Buckinghamshire have investigated life in the Second World War (1939-1945) and talked to those who remember it about their experience and memories. The results of their project are on www.livingarchive.org.uk *This is what they have uncovered about clothes of the 1940s.*

1   The clothing industry was a lot smaller during the war and clothes became more expensive. To make sure everyone could afford them, the government introduced 'Utility Clothing'. This was made from a particular cloth and cut in a special way so only the smallest amount was used.

5   Clothing rationing was introduced in June 1941 and operated on a 'points' basis. Each person was allowed 66 clothing coupons a year. For example:

> Man's suit – 26 coupons
> Woollen dress – 11 coupons
> Child's shoes – 3 coupons

10   People were encouraged to 'make do and mend' by the government who suggested ways to revamp old clothes. Patching and darning meant clothes could be worn for longer.

Boys aged 4-14 in the 1930s and '40s would normally have worn:

> Short trousers
15
> Shirt and tie (usually a knitted school tie)
> V-necked jumper
> Jacket or school blazer
> Long socks
> Sandals or boots

20   Girls aged 4-14 in the 1930s and '40s would normally have worn:

> Cotton frock (dress) in summer
> Gym-slip and blouse in winter
> Cardigan or jumper
25
> School beret or hat
> Long socks or lisle[1] stockings
> Sandals or shoes

Monica Austin remembers: 'We used to have Thermojene inside our clothes. It was a kind of orange cotton wool, stronger than cotton wool but it kept the warmth on your
30   chest. We used to put it down as we got dressed to keep us warm.'

Note:
[1] Lisle: a type of thread

Exercise 4.2

Read the information on 'Utility clothing' and answer these questions as fully as you can:

1. What was 'Utility Clothing' (line 3)?

2. What did people do to make their clothes last longer?

3. Explain in your own words what Thermojene was (line 28).

4. Why do you think the government introduced a 'points' system?

5. What would Chas McGill probably have been wearing?

Exercise 4.3

Your turn to write:

1. Chas McGill collected war souvenirs. Write in any way you wish about something that you collect.

2. Write about an occasion when you have seen or found something which has surprised, frightened or puzzled you.

3. Describe in detail, and in your own words, the appearance of a 10-year-old school girl or boy in the 1940s. Introduce extra details to make your writing as lively as possible.

4. Imagine you are a journalist on Chas McGill's local paper. You've interviewed him about his find in the wood. Write your report for the paper.

5. Write in any way you wish about war.

Grammar and punctuation

Exclamation marks

An exclamation mark (**!**) draws attention to a sentence which is more dramatic than a plain sentence which ends in a full stop. It is often used to show that the sentence is (or is supposed to be) funny. It should not be used too often. Don't use more than one at a time, and remember, an exclamation mark stands on its own. You don't need any other mark of punctuation with it.

For example:

> My teacher came to school wearing a green wig!
> There are seven girls named Charlotte in my class!
> I have read *The Machine Gunners* eleven times!
> What a lovely book!

An exclamation mark

You also need an exclamation mark after a single word or short exclamation such as:

> Cool!   Great!   Oh dear!   Good heavens!

Exercise 4.4

Exclamation mark activities:

1.　Punctuate the following exclamations:
   (a) stop thief
   (b) what a terrible story
   (c) how hot the weather is
   (d) you poor child
   (e) what a shame
   (f) how lovely

2.　Write out the following, correctly punctuated. Some are exclamations. Some are ordinary sentences.
   (a) he wanted to find the source of the smell
   (b) how few clothes those children had in the 1940s
   (c) no don't do that
   (d) most girls wore berets
   (e) mending clothes made them last
   (f) what a smell
   (g) ouch

Adverbs

An adverb is a word which tells you more about another word, usually a verb. It **qualifies** or **modifies** it. Adverbs often tell you **how** or **when** something happened. Many adverbs, but not all, end in '-ly'. For example:

> He picked himself up **quickly**.

> His right eye, pale grey, watched through the goggle glass, **tolerantly** and a little **sadly**.

> Monica Austin remembers Thermojene **well**.

> I shall do my prep **soon**.

An adverb qualifying a verb

Exercise 4.5

Adverb activities:

1. Put adverbs into these sentences:

    (a) Chas McGill entered the wood ... and searched ... for souvenirs.

    (b) During the war everyone had to dress ...

    (c) Many people are now ... interested in the Second World War.

    (d) Children in the war were ... advised to keep away from aircraft and weapons.

    (e) Some older people ... remember Second World War bombing raids ...

    (f) Rationing was a way of sharing things out ...

2. Most adjectives (see Chapter 3) which qualify or modify nouns can be converted into adverbs which qualify or modify verbs. Make these adjectives into adverbs. Some have been done for you.

Adjective	Adverb
normal	...
good	well
funny	funnily
bad	...
expensive	...
frightening	...
public	publicly
clear	...
warm	...
easy	...

Now use each of the adverbs above in a sentence of your own.

Vocabulary and spelling

1. **Utility** means usefulness. During the Second World War people were encouraged to buy specially-made cheap and simple utility furniture and other items, as well as clothing.

    A **utility room** in a house is one where useful jobs such as washing clothes are done. In sport a **utilty player** is one who can usefully play well in any one of several positions.

    Futility means uselessness or without usefulness.

2. **Thermojene** was the name give to a substance which helped to keep people warm in the 1940s. Any word containing 'therm' has something to do with heat. It comes from *thermos*, the Ancient Greek word for 'heat'.

    A **thermometer** measures heat.

    Thermal clothing keeps you especially warm.

    A **thermos** flask is a special container which keeps liquids hot, perhaps for picnics.

Look at a good dictionary for many other – mainly scientific – words containing 'therm'.

3.   Look at the spelling of **retrieve**. The 'i' comes before the 'e' because the sound that it is making is 'eee' as in 'feel', not 'aiii' as in 'file'. Learn these:

achieve	believe	relief	niece	piece
field	siege	pier	thief	grief

But beware! When a 'c' comes first, the 'e' and 'i' change places. So:

conceit
deceive
receive
ceiling

But note that this rule only applies when the sound is 'eee', as in the words above.

4.   When you form an adverb from an adjective ending with a 'y' the rule is that the 'y' changes to an 'i' before 'ly' is added.

So:

funny	funnily
merry	merrily
happy	happily
silky	silkily
hungry	hungrily

Remember: 'i' before 'e', except after 'c'.

Remember: Change 'y' to 'i' and add 'ly'.

Collect and list as many examples of this rule as you can.

Speaking and listening

1.   Read one or more of the books listed below. Read a short extract from it aloud to your class and tell the rest of the group what you liked or disliked about the book.

2.   Working with a partner, make up a conversation between a child of your age from the 1940s and one from the 21st century. Talk about what you each do in your spare time, what you wear and anything else that interests you. Then perform your conversation to the rest of the class.

3.   Discuss war in groups. When, if ever, is it right? When, if ever, is it wrong? Why do people go to war? What effect does it have on ordinary people across the world? A spokesman for your group could then explain your group's views to the rest of the class.

Have you read?

All these are about children and how they were affected by the Second World War in Britain and elsewhere:

The Machine Gunners by Robert Westall (Macmillan 2001 reprint)
Back Home by Michelle Magorian (Puffin 1987)
The Diary of a Young Girl by Anne Frank (Puffin Modern Classics 2002)
Carrie's War by Nina Bawden (Puffin Modern Classics 1993 reprint)
Fireweed by Jill Paton Walsh (Farrar Strauss and Giroux 1988)
The Silver Sword by Ian Seraillier (Red Fox 2003 reprint)
August '44 by Carlo Gebler (Egmont 2003)
Mischling Second Degree by Ilse Koehn (Penguin 2003 reprint)
The Endless Steppe by Esther Hautzig (HarperTrophy 1995 reprint)
The Exeter Blitz by David Rees (Heinemann Windmills 1981)

And if you've done all that

● Sir Winston Churchill was Britain's Prime Minister during the Second World War. He made some very famous speeches to encourage people to be strong. They were broadcast on radio. Get a tape or CD of these speeches (from your local library or www.amazon.co.uk or www.churchill-society-london.org.uk). What do you learn from them about (a) how British people must then have been feeling; and (b) Churchill's personality?

● Find out what you can about Robert Westall who wrote *The Machine Gunners*. Write a short account of his life and work for display in your classroom.

● Look through some anthologies of 20th century poetry to find poems about the Second World War. Write some of them out to form your own anthology.

Chapter 5

On stage

Nat Field is an American boy who has come to London in 1999 to take part in a children's production of Shakespeare's 'A Midsummer Night's Dream' at the new Globe Theatre. Taken seriously ill, he finds himself transported back to the old Globe Theatre four hundred years earlier.

1   'There it is – our new theatre!' said Harry proudly. 'Hast seen it before?'

'No,' I said truthfully, staring. A white flag was flying from the flagpole on the top of the Globe, the signal to audiences that a play would be done there that day. For the moment it was the only thing I recognised. It wasn't the theatre itself that was so

5   different from the copy that would be built in my time; it was the surroundings. This Globe wasn't crowded and dwarfed by towering office buildings; it stood up proud and high, and to the south it looked out over green fields and billowing trees. In fact there were trees nearly all round it. Once we had left the main street that went over London Bridge, I'd felt with astonishment that we were walking into the countryside. The streets

10   were still busy and noisy, though with carts and coaches and horsemen and others like us bustling on foot.

Like the Globe of my own time, the theatre looked new; its plaster gleamed white, the reeds of its thatch lay tight and straight-edged. As Harry chattered proudly on, I realised it really was new, finished only a few months earlier. Before that, the company had been

15   playing for years in a theatre – called, believe it or not, just The Theatre – across the river in Shoreditch, until their lease on the land ran out and the landlord refused to renew it. Master Burbage and his brother Cuthbert had just inherited The Theatre from their father James who built it. There it stood, useless, on ground they weren't allowed to set foot on. Where were they to act?

20   'It was the actors who solved the problem,' Harry said, grinning. Five of them got together with the Burbages, raised enough money to lease a piece of land here in Southwark, and hired a master carpenter. Then, one dark winter's night just after Christmas, taking a dozen strong workmen with them, they went quietly to Shoreditch and with axes and sledgehammers and crowbars they took The Theatre apart. They did it very carefully,

25   numbering each piece, and it took them three days. The demolition must have been a very noisy process, but Harry said that not many people lived in the area close by.

After that they had carted all The Theatre's major beams and timbers to the River Thames – huge oak beams Harry said, some of them thirty feet long – and shipped them over to the other side. And there, using them for a framework, the workmen gradually

30   built the theatre that they christened the Globe.

Birds were singing in the trees outside the theatre as we went in. The doors seemed smaller than in my day, and in different places, so that I couldn't tell whether we were headed backstage or for the groundlings' pit. I followed Harry and Burbage blindly. The whole theatre had an odd musty, grassy smell that I couldn't place and everywhere, of

35 course, there were unfamiliar accents and clothes. To keep from thinking I was crazy, I'd begun to pretend that I was in the middle of a movie set in Elizabethan times, among actors dressed in costume. It was comforting until something screamingly real hit me, like those heads on London Bridge.

There was a bright light ahead of us all at once. Master Burbage paused and I found we

40 had come out on to the central little balcony at the back of the stage. Ahead and around us were the empty galleries of the theatre; above us the painted sky of the 'heavens' that gave the stage its roof and below on the broad, thrusting stage two figures, arguing.

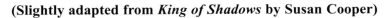

(Slightly adapted from *King of Shadows* by Susan Cooper)

The Globe Theatre

Exercise 5.1

Read the extract from *King of Shadows* and answer the following questions:

1. List three differences Nat notices between the 20th century Globe Theatre he knows and the old one he has been transported back to.

2. Who built The Theatre in Shoreditch?

3. Why could The Theatre no longer be used?

4. Give another word for (a) demolition (line 25) and (b) musty (line 34).

5. In order to travel from Shoreditch to Southwark what must you cross?

6. Why do the people in the theatre look and sound odd to Nat?

The modern Globe

Now read this factual information about the building of the Globe Theatre in the 1990s:

1   Since its opening in 1997 the new Globe Theatre has become a successful performance
       space and London's leading tourist attraction.

       For nearly a decade McCurdy & Co. were closely involved in the authentic
       reconstruction of Shakespeare's original 'wooden O', carrying out much of the early
5   research and analysis, together with the detailed design and fabrication of the entire
       oak frame.

       Peter McCurdy and his team of craftsmen were selected for the project after Sam
       Wanamaker[1] had seen McCurdy & Co. at work on the reconstruction of Barley Hall, a
       14th-century timber-framed building in the centre of York.

10   As there were no building records in existence, the Globe team had to rely on historic
       reference material and on Peter McCurdy's own knowledge of carpentry, methodology
       of the period and analysis of the relevant contemporary buildings to help determine the
       overall design. Then, in keeping with tradition, the phased fabrication of the oak frame
       was carried out off-site at McCurdy's own Berkshire workshops. The shaped timbers
15   were then transported to site for erection.

       The greatest challenge was resolving the design for the complex stage and tiring house[2].
       Peter McCurdy spent six months surveying timber structures to find historic precedents
       and also sourcing suitable oak trees from which to shape the 28 foot columns and cross
       beam supporting the 16 tonne roof.

20   The Globe Education Trust is now actively promoting the theatre worldwide as a centre
       for research, education and dramatic training.

(Taken from website of McCurdy and Co. www.mccurdyco.com)

Notes:
[1] American actor, a supporter of the new Globe Theatre in London
[2] Dressing room

Exercise 5.2

Read the extract 'The modern Globe' and answer the following questions:

1.   How long has the new Globe Theatre been open?

2.   What was the most difficult part of Peter McCurdy's job?

3.   Why did Sam Wanamaker choose Peter McCurdy for this work?

4.   Where was most of the work done?

5.   Describe the theatre's structure in your own words and in as much detail as you can.

6.   This passage mentions five different jobs that the new Globe Theatre now does. List them.

Exercise 5.3

Your turn to write:

1.   Write a story about someone who moves to a time other than his or her own.

2.   Imagine you are a journalist interviewing Nat Field when he returns to the present day. Write your article for a newspaper or magazine.

3.   Write on the subject of theatre in any way you wish.

4.   Write a review for a newspaper or magazine of any play, musical, pantomime or film you have seen recently. Include how it was done, which actors did well and which less well. Say what you liked and disliked about the production.

5.   Write an account of any school (or other) play you have taken part in. Include as much detail as you can. For example: How did you rehearse? How did you feel when you got your part? What were the costumes like? How did it go when you performed it for an audience?

Grammar and punctuation

Adjectives from nouns

Nouns and adjective are often versions of the same word:

Noun	Adjective
theatre	theatrical
Britain	British
bird	birdlike
grass	grassy
history	historical
education	educational

There are patterns that you can see, but great care needs to be taken with the spelling. For example, in many cases we add '-ful' (note **one** 'l', not two):

truth	truthful
wonder	wonderful
cheer	cheerful

Or we can add 'y' (or 'ly'):

craft	crafty
love	lovely
noise	noisy

These patterns are easy enough for people who have been speaking English all their lives, but pity those who have to learn English as a foreign language! Truthful? truthy? truthlike? truthly? Not easy!

Exercise 5.4

Noun/adjective activities:

Adjectives being formed from nouns

1. Write a list of as many nouns ending in '–iness' as you can. List corresponding adjectives based on them.

2. Write a list of as many adjectives ending '–y' as you can. List corresponding nouns next to them.

3. Put the right noun or adjective in the following sentences:

   (a) The Globe is a (carefulness/careful) replica of an (Elizabethan/Elizabeth) building.

   (b) We can understand the (popular/popularity) of (Shakespeare/Shakespearian) drama.

   (c) Nat Field was surprised by the (atmosphere/atmospheric) of Tudor London.

   (d) Shakespeare was (English/England).

   (e) Oak is a very (hardness/hard) and (reliable/reliability) wood.

Hyphens

A hyphen is a small horizontal line which separates two or more linked words, or parts of a word. When we use more than one word to form a single idea we need a hyphen:

pre-war theatre
under-11 netball team
end-of-term report

A hyphen

Hyphens change the way we say things. Practise saying aloud: 'Let's take away that rubbish!' and 'Let's get a take-away supper!' Can you hear the difference?

Hyphens also make meaning clearer.
For example:

King Henry VIII married his sister-in-law.
Nat Field was a twelve-year-old boy when he came to London.
Prince Charles is an ex-naval officer.

Exercise 5.5

Put hyphens into these sentences:

1. We put on a play with a five person cast.

2. King James I of England was a non smoker.

3. In Shakespeare's play *Hamlet*, Claudius is Gertrude's brother in law as well as her new husband and Hamlet's stepfather.

4. *Henry V* by Shakespeare, written in 1599, was a turn of the century play.

5. Queen Victoria's end of reign celebration was her Diamond Jubilee in 1897 when she had been monarch for 60 years.

6. Shakespeare lived in Stratford upon Avon.

Dashes

All sentences must have a capital letter at the beginning and a full stop, question or exclamation mark at the end, but you can sometimes use a dash within the sentence to break up the meaning. A dash looks exactly like a hyphen but is not attached to a particular word.

For example:

> There it is – our new theatre.
> Queen Victoria had nine children – then her husband died.
> Charles I upset his subjects – so they beheaded him.

A dash (cutting a dash)

Exercise 5.6

Put dashes into these sentences:

1. The Globe Theatre was magnificent but it burnt down.

2. Shakespeare's Macbeth was very ambitious although audiences usually think he was led on by his wife.

3. Sam Wanamaker worked for years on the Globe Theatre project but died before it was finished.

4. Queen Elizabeth encouraged playwrights but she never went to the theatre.

Did you know?

You can use dashes in pairs, like brackets:

> William Shakespeare – a remarkable playwright – wrote both tragedies and comedies.
> A magnificent palace on the Thames – Hampton Court – was given to Henry VIII by Thomas Wolsey.

Vocabulary and spelling

1. When The Theatre was dismantled, craftsmen had to number the pieces **carefully**. The following adverbs are similar in meaning to **carefully**:

    scrupulously   delicately
    meticulously   attentively
    painstakingly

    Look up their precise meaning and use them in sentences of your own.

2. If you **fabricate** something, as Peter McCurdy's staff did the oak structure of the new Globe Theatre, you **make** it.

    Look up and list short (one sound or one syllable) words for the following longer ones:

    veracity   peregrination
    endeavour   obtain
    purchase   ingest

    A famous newspaper editor, Harold Evans, advised his writers never to use a long word where a short one would do. It's good advice. Although you need to know the meaning of as many longer words as possible, it's often better to use the shortest possible one in your writing.

3. Many abstract nouns end in '–ness' but take care with the spelling of two groups. First, if the adjective from which the noun is formed ends in 'n' then adding '–ness' means that the word is spelt with a double 'n'. Fear not; this is correct.

For example: 'open' becomes 'openness' and 'clean' becomes 'cleanness'.

Learn these:

sternness   suddenness
drunkenness   keenness
sullenness   meanness
leanness   greenness
thinness   woodenness

Second. If the adjective from which the noun is formed ends in 'y' then the 'y' changes to an 'i' before '–ness' is added.

For example: 'tiny' becomes 'tininess' and 'fussy' becomes 'fussiness'.

Learn these:

tidiness   silliness
happiness   noisiness
crankiness   worthiness
dizziness   weariness
readiness   sulkiness

Speaking and listening

1. Work in a group. Make up a short play in which a modern person meets one or more characters from the past.

2. Shakespeare wrote 150 sonnets (14 line poems). Find one which you like. Practise reading it aloud. Hold a class 'Sonnet Festival' in which you all perform your sonnets.

3. Work out your own short version of the story of any of Shakespeare's plays. Retell it to a small group.

4. Prepare a short talk for the rest of the class on any aspect of theatre, history or building.

Have you read?

All these are about the theatre, plays or Shakespeare:

King of Shadows by Susan Cooper (Puffin 2000)
Stratford Boys by Jan Mark (Hodder Children's paperback 2004)
The Swish of the Curtain by Pamela Brown (Hodder Children's Books 1995)
Shakespeare Stories by Leon Garfield (Puffin 1997)
Shakespeare Stories II by Leon Garfield (Puffin 1997)
The Dark Behind the Curtain by Gillian Cross (OUP 2001)
Ballet Shoes by Noel Streatfeild (Puffin Modern Classics 1994)
Theatre Shoes by Noel Streatfeild (Hodder Children's paperback 1995)
A Spoonful of Jam by Michelle Magorian (Mammoth 1998)
Billy Elliot by Melvyn Burgess, based on motion picture screenplay by Lee Hall
        (Chicken House 2001)
Stagestruck by Adèle Geras (Piccadilly 1999)
Lights, Camera, Action! by Adèle Geras (Piccadilly 2000)

And if you've done all that

●   In the extract from *King of Shadows*, Nat Field remembered 'those heads on London Bridge' (line 38). Find out what this refers to. Use reference books or the Internet. Share what you've found out with the rest of the class.

●   Find out how many plays Shakespeare wrote. Design a large poster listing them all, or most of them, with a sentence or two and an illustration for each. Work out how best to group or list them. Display it in the classroom or elsewhere in the school. (Leon Garfield's books could help with this. See 'Have you read?' above.)

●   Read, or try to see a production or film of, *A Midsummer Night's Dream*. Then design costumes and sets for an imaginative production of your own.

Chapter 6

Fantasy

Phoenix is exploring the Greek myth 'Theseus and the Minotaur' in a very realistic and dangerous way.

1   But still the beast stood in the archway, pawing at the floor. It was bigger than a man.
    It stood almost three metres tall and was massively built with slabs of muscle on its
    chest and shoulders. Below the waist it was bull-like. It had a swinging tail and mud-
    splattered hooves. Or was it mud? Above the waist it was a man, except, that is, for the

5   head. And what a head! The muzzle was huge and when it opened, it revealed the sharp,
    curved teeth, not of a bull but of a big cat. They were the fangs of a lion or tiger made
    for ripping flesh. Its eyes were yellow and blazed unflinchingly through the murk. Then
    there were the great horns, glinting and sharp, curving from its monstrous brow. Thick
    and muscular as the neck was, it seemed barely able to support such a fearsome head,

10 and strained visibly under the impossible weight.

    'Oh my!'

    The beast stepped out from the tunnel and the boy actually took a few steps back. It was
    as if his soul had crept out of his body and was tugging at him, begging him to get
    away. In the sparse light shed from the gratings in the ceiling the beast looked even

15 more hideous. There was sweat for a start, standing out in gleaming beads on that
    enormous neck and shoulders.

    But that wasn't all. The creature was smeared from head to foot with filth and dried
    blood. It was every inch a killer. The beast began to stamp forward, its hooves clashing
    on the stone floor. It raised its head, the horns scraping on the ceiling and gave a bellow

20 that seemed to crush the air.

    'I can't do this . . .'

    He fell back, scrambling over the obstacles on the floor and fled. That's when he
    realised he'd dropped his ball of string. His lifeline had gone.

    'Oh no!'

25 The beast was charging head down.

    Got to get out of here!

    In his mind's eye, he could see himself impaled on the points of those evil-looking horns, his
    legs pedalling feebly in the air, his head snapped back, his eyes growing pale and lifeless.

    Suddenly he was running for his life, skidding on the slimy floor.

    * * * * * *

30   Ripping off the mask and gloves, Phoenix bent
        double, gulping down air like it had been
        rationed. The dank half-light of the tunnels
        was replaced by the welcome glow from
        an Anglepoise lamp in his father's study.
35   He glanced at the score bracelet on his
        wrist. It registered total defeat:
        000000. For a few moments
        everything was spinning, the claws of
        the game digging into the flesh of the
40   here and now. Then his surroundings
        became reassuringly familiar.

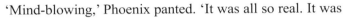

He was out. It was a game.

'Well?' his dad asked. 'What do you think?'

'Mind-blowing,' Phoenix panted. 'It was all so real. It was
45   like another world. I mean I *was* Theseus. I went into the palace of the tyrant-king Minos.
        I could actually touch the stone columns, feel the heat of the braziers, smell the incense.'

He knew he was gushing, babbling like a little kid, but he didn't care. 'The king's
daughter Ariadne helped me and she wasn't just an image on a screen. She was a real
girl. Then I actually came face to face with the Minotaur. It was really happening.
50   I believed it,' he shivered. 'Still do.'

'Oh I could tell how convincing it was,' said Dad, enjoying the mixture of excitement
and fear in his son's voice. 'You were screaming your silly head off by the end. I bet
your mother thought I was killing you in here.'

(From *Shadow of the Minotaur* by Alan Gibbons)

Exercise 6.1

Read the extract from *Shadow of the Minotaur* and answer these questions:

1.   Describe the beast as accurately as you can using your own words.

2.   Give another word for (a) sparse (line 14), (b) impaled (line 27) and (c) braziers (line 46).

3.   Phoenix experiences the beast's world with four of his five senses (sight, hearing, touch, smell). How do we know this?

4.   How did Phoenix feel when he found himself in his father's study?

5.   Why did the score bracelet show a row of zeros (or noughts) (line 37)?

6.   What sort of game do you think Phoenix is playing?

His Dark Materials: a review

This is a theatre review. The author has seen the two plays and then written her views in a newspaper.

1   *His Dark Materials*
        Olivier, National Theatre

Author:	Philip Pullman, adapted by Nicholas Wright
Director:	Nicholas Hytner
5	**Cast includes**:	Anna Maxwell Martin, Dominic Cooper, Patricia Hodge, Timothy Dalton, Niamh Cusack
Running time:	Part one 3 hrs 5mins, Part two 3 hrs 10mins

The epic grandiloquence of Philip Pullman's novels, upon which *His Dark Materials* is based, makes this two-part play one of the most ambitious projects ever undertaken in
10 the theatre. But how Nick Hytner and his team bring it off!

The whole thrums with theatrical tension, ideas, action and spectacle throughout two substantial plays. The 'good versus evil' plot weaves between worlds from quasi-medieval Oxford, repressively controlled by chilling Catholic clerics, to 21st century traffic-clogged Oxford. Threaded between are other geographical locations both real and
15 imaginary – from the Arctic populated by splendidly masked armoured bears, witches and other forces to a grey harpy-run Hell.

Rarely can the Olivier's full revolve, operating in several planes to reveal set after set, have been so imaginatively used. It's almost filmic – the curtain call, taken by the 50-plus back-stage crew at the end is richly deserved.

20 In Pullman's fictional worlds of *His Dark Materials* most humans are attached to personal daemons – animal-shaped physical manifestations of the individual soul. Glowing, never-still puppets are lithely operated, Japanese-style, by masked black-clad shadows. The daemons add unexpected dramatic depth – their reactions are, effectively a sub-textual commentary on the thoughts of their alter egos.

25 At the heart of all this is the remarkable Anna Maxwell Martin, only 18 months out of LAMDA[1] playing the 12-year-old Lyra. An outstanding actress with an assured future before her, she brings to the part a combination of mercurial intensity, truculence, passion and waspish humour.

Well supported by the sensitively gravelly Dominic Cooper as Will Parry, Maxwell
30 Martin adeptly sustains Lyra's magnetism for over six hours in this huge and demanding Hamlet-scale role.

Patricia Hodge turns in a characteristically assured performance as Lyra's crisp mother, Mrs Coulter, who starts off pretty evil but eventually achieves a redemption of sorts. And Niamh Cusack makes a breathy, high-voiced chief witch quite convincing, if a bit

35   thin on range. Timothy Dalton, however, tends to woodenness and is sometimes guilty
of gabbling his words as Lord Asriel, especially in Part One.

Jonathan Dove's atmospheric music for an eight-piece band, immaculately led by
Stephen Ellis, is yet another highly successful strand in this deeply-moving, profound
but also gloriously entertaining production.

(Review by Susan Elkin, published in *The Stage*, 08 January 2004)

Note:
[1] London Academy of Music and Dramatic Art – a training school for actors

Exercise 6.2

Read the review of *His Dark Materials* and then answer these questions:

1.   Part 2 of *His Dark Materials* begins at 7.00 pm. What time does it end?

2.   What part does Anna Maxwell Martin play?

3.   List (a) every adjective and (b) every adverb in this passage which tell you that the
reviewer enjoyed this pair of plays.

4.   What two aspects of it did she not like and why?

5.   How are the characters' daemons shown on stage?

6.   What special feature of the Olivier Theatre made the plays particularly effective and
why?

Exercise 6.3

Your turn to write:

1.   Invent a terrible beast and write the story of a human's encounter with it.

2.   Write a review of any play (or film) that you have seen recently.

3.   Retell in your own words any story you already know about humans battling to defeat
frightening beasts (such as St George and the Dragon, Daniel in the Lions' Den or Red
Riding Hood). Make it as vivid as you can.

4.   Write any kind of story which either of the two extracts above suggests to you.

5.   Design an advertising leaflet to persuade people to buy tickets for *His Dark Materials*.
Use the information in the review.

6.   Do you like reading fantasy books? Write an essay explaining your views. (It doesn't
matter whether you're a fantasy fan or a fantasy hater!) Mention books that you have
read or seen as films.

Grammar and punctuation

Apostrophes

The apostrophe – that little hanging comma above the line – has two main jobs:

First it stands in for a letter or group of letters which has been left out.

> **Wouldn't** is short for 'would not'.
> **M'chester** (on a sign post) is short for 'Manchester'.
> **O'clock** is short for 'of the clock' which is what people used to say.
> **It's** is short for 'it is' or 'it has'.
> **I'm** is short for 'I am'.

An apostrophe

Exercise 6.4

1. Link these shortened forms (a-h) with their full versions (i-viii):

   (a) C'bury   (i) is not
   (b) can't   (ii) there is
   (c) let's   (iii) Peterborough
   (d) P'boro   (iv) who is
   (e) there's   (v) cannot
   (f) you'll   (vi) let us
   (g) who's   (vii) Canterbury
   (h) isn't   (viii) you will

2. Six apostrophes have been left out of the following passage. Your job is to put them in.

   Abigail knew shed have to hurry. Shed been told to get to the shop before it shut at six oclock. 'Weve run out of salt,' she told Mr Evans, the corner shopkeeper. 'Were having fish and chips for supper and itd be horrible without salt.'

Apostrophes (cont.)

The second job of the apostrophe is to show the 'owner' of something. There are four basic rules:

1. The apostrophe is added to the noun naming the owner.
2. The apostrophe goes before the 's' if the naming noun is singular (only one).
3. The apostrophe goes after the 's' if the naming noun is plural (more than one).
4. It makes no difference if the naming noun already ends in 's' or even 'ss'.

So:

The caves owned by the Minotaur are the **Minotaur's caves.**
The books owned by 29 boys are the **boys' books**
The dog owned by Marcus is **Marcus's** dog.
The costume worn by an actress is an **actress's costume.**

Do not get into the habit of scattering apostrophes in your writing every time you use an **'s'**!

You have to think quite hard every time. In the following sentence the letter 's' is sometimes connected with an apostrophe and sometimes not:

Sarah's sisters left their **neighbours'** dogs tied to two posts outside Safeway while they went inside to buy two boxes of chocolates for their **aunt's** birthday.

Exercise 6.5

Rewrite the following using an apostrophe:

e.g. The books written by Philip Pullman = Philip Pullman's books

1.   The script owned by Timothy Dalton
2.   The huge horns of the Minotaur
3.   The computer game used by my brother
4.   The father of Phoenix
5.   The play written by Nicholas Wright
6.   The big bag of crisps bought for all the boys
7.   The coat worn by the princess
8.   The sister of the princesses

Adjectives for comparing

An adjective may be **compared** in three degrees: positive, comparative and superlative:

Positive	Comparative	Superlative
fierce	fiercer	fiercest
pale	paler	palest
tiny	tinier	tiniest
enjoyable	more enjoyable	most enjoyable
frightening	more frightening	most frightening
good	better	best
bad	worse	worst

Most short adjectives take '–er' and '–est', sometimes with a slight change in spelling (such as 'easy-easier-easiest'). Longer adjectives need 'more' or 'most' in front of them. Exceptions such as 'good-better-best' are relatively rare and just have to be learned.

Exercise 6.6

Comparative adjectives activities:

1. Write a list of ten adjectives. Write the comparative and superlative forms next to them.

2. Put the right comparative or superlative adjectives in these sentences:
    (a) The koala bear is the ... (sweet) little bear in the world.
    (b) London is ... (crowded) than Edinburgh.
    (c) *Shadow of the Minotaur* is the ... (exciting) fantasy I have read.
    (d) The Olivier is one of London's ... (large) theatres.
    (e) *His Dark Materials* is the ... (good) thing Philip Pullman has written.
    (f) This slave girl is pretty, this one is quite attractive but this one over here is by far the ... (beautiful).

Vocabulary and spelling

1. The Minotaur in the Greek myth was part-man and part-bull. *Taurus* is Latin for a bull. *Tauros* is Ancient Greek for a bull.

    Taurine is an adjective meaning bull-like. So: The gigantic **taurine** head reared over Theseus.

    Taurus, the bull, is the name given to a bull-shaped group of stars.

    Taurus, the bull, is the second sign of the zodiac. Astrologers believe that people born between April 20 and May 20 are influenced by this sign. (Look up and learn the difference between an **astronomer** and an **astrologer**.)

    Tauromachy is another word for bull fighting.

2. **Grandiloquent** means grandly spoken. It comes from the Latin word *loquor* which means *I speak*.

3. **Muzzle** is spelt with a double z. Learn also:

guzzle	puzzle
embezzle	sizzle
nuzzle	dazzle
drizzle	

4. **Monstrous** is an adjective formed from the noun 'monster' – but, unusually, the adjective has no 'e'. Learn also:

    disastrous (from disaster)
    wondrous (from wonder)
    leprous (from leper)

5. **Historical** is the adjective formed from history. Learn also:

    geographical (from geography)
    biological (from biology)
    philosophical (from philosophy)
    geometrical (from geometry)

Work with a partner and test each other. Remember it's much more important to be able to write a word down correctly than to spell it aloud.

Exercise 6.7

Vocabulary activity:

Find out what the following words – all from *loquor* (= I speak) – mean and use them in sentences of your own:
1. eloquent
2. loquacious
3. ventriloquist

Speaking and listening

1. Work in a group of three or four. Prepare a shared reading of the extract from *Shadow of the Minotaur*. Make it as dramatic as you can. Perform your reading to another group.

2. Organise formal class discussions on (a) 'Are computer games a good thing?' and (b) 'Why do so many children and young people like fantasy?'

3. Look through some anthologies of poetry. Choose a poem – or part of one – which you like, perhaps with a fantasy theme. Learn it by heart. Perform it for the others in your class.

4. Work in a pair. Pretend that one of you loves reading and the other hates it. Decide who is to take which point of view – it doesn't matter what you really think. Work out your arguments and see if you can persuade your partner to agree with you.

Have you read?

These books are all fantasies to some extent:

Shadow of the Minotaur by Alan Gibbons (Orion 2000)
His Dark Materials (trilogy) by Philip Pullman (Scholastic Point 2001)
The Wonderful Wizard of Oz by Frank L Baum (Penguin Popular Classics 1995)
The Amazing Maurice and his Educated Rodents by Terry Pratchett (Corgi 2001)
Alice in Wonderland by Lewis Carroll (Penguin Popular Classics 1994)
The Doomspell by Cliff McNish (Orion 2001)
The Lion, the Witch and the Wardrobe by CS Lewis, illustrated by Pauline Baynes
    (Picture Lions, 2003 edition)
The Witches by Roald Dahl (Puffin 2001)
Space Race by Sylvia Waugh (Yearling Books 2001)
The Earthsea Quartet by Ursula K Le Guin (Puffin 1993)
The Wind Singer by William Nicholson (Egmont 2003)
Grinny by Nicholas Fisk (Puffin Modern Classics 1996)
Elidor by Alan Garner (Collins Modern Classics 2001)
Mrs Frisby and the Rats of NIMH by Robert O'Brien (Puffin Modern Classics 1994)
Skellig by David Almond (Hodder 1999)

And if you've done all that

● Take a short story you know and like (it could also be a fairy story, folk tale or myth). Adapt it as a play. You could write out the scripts by hand or word process them on a computer. Get a group of friends to perform your play for the rest of the class.

● Conduct a survey of some children and adults to find out what they think about fantasy and whether they like it or not. Find a way of making your findings clear (e.g. in a graph or table) and display them on a wall poster.

● Is fantasy better in books than in plays and films? Work out your views and the reasons for them. Write a letter to Philip Pullman or to JK Rowling, author of the Harry Potter books, or any other writer of a fantasy that you've read, expressing your opinion.

Chapter 7

Hot spots

Flora and her mother have travelled to North Borneo where her father is to work. It is the 1950s. This passage describes some of her first impressions.

1 'I can hear the sea,' I said. 'Is it far away?'

'Far away?' Dad laughed. 'It's just behind those trees. Finish your drink and come and see.'

'She's tired, dear,' said Mum. 'Won't tomorrow do?'

5 Dad said: 'It's not far, really. Two hundred yards at the most. Why don't you come too?'

'No you go, and I'll unpack. It'll wait for me until tomorrow.'

'Right Flora. Take your socks off, but keep your sandals on until we get to the beach. Don't want you stepping on any snakes.'

'Snakes? Really?'

10 'Yes, and every other kind of creepy-crawly you can think of. But we won't leave the path, and we'll be very careful, I promise. You'll have to get used to it.'

'Are they poisonous, Dad?'

'Some are and some aren't, I daresay, but you shouldn't stop to enquire.'

Green. Green everywhere. Thick, moist, dark. Palm trees, fronds, vines, ferns uncurling
15 in small spots of sunlight filtering through the overhanging leaves. At the end of the green tunnel, sand like talcum powder blew under my feet. There was the sea, royal blue, turquoise, aquamarine, clear emerald, cloudy jade: all the blues and greens in the world lying in swirls and stripes from the shore to the horizon. Waves spread themselves out, one after another, on the sand, like pretty skirts frilled with white crochet.

20 We found a jellyfish, washed up on the damp shore, a horrible pinkish and blueish and greyish creature like left-over jelly at a party, all blobby and soft. I poked it about with a stick. Afterwards I felt very sorry that I had. Poor jellyfish. I wouldn't like to have all my squashy bits prodded like that, even if I were dead.

There was no long twilight. The sun plunged into the waves, unfurling scarlet and gold
25 streamers into the sky behind it; and once it had gone, the colours faded to lilac, then to darkness. By the time we returned to the house, night had fallen.

'Have we ever had any snakes? In the house?' My voice felt shaky.

'Not while I've been here. But always shake your shoes and slippers before you put them on. Make sure no nasties have crawled inside.'

30   'Nasties? What nasties?'

'Scorpions, for instance.'

Scorpions in my slippers! I really wished at that moment that I could be back in England again.

35   That first night, I couldn't fall asleep for a long time. I lay for a while in bed under the white veils of my mosquito net, looking at the outlines of everyday things blurred by darkness and the misty walls of my small tent. I heard my mother turning out the lights in the lounge and soon there was only a faint yellow glow from the half-open door of my parents' bedroom. The night was loud with insect noises, the sound of a million unseen wings in the long grass under the house and in the black shapes of the trees behind it.

(Slightly abridged from *Other Echoes* by Adèle Geras)

Exercise 7.1

Read the extract from *Other Echoes* and answer these questions as fully as you can:

1.   Roughly how long would it have taken Flora and her father to walk to the sea?

2.   What will Flora's mother do while her husband and daughter are out?

3.   What is Flora most frightened of and why?

4.   Why does she regret her treatment of the jellyfish?

5.   How could you tell from this passage, even if you had not been told, that Flora is not a 21st century child?

6.   How is dusk in Borneo different from dusk in England?

7.   What keeps Flora awake?

An Indian Ocean Odyssey

Advertisement

1

A great value voyage of discovery to some of the most fascinating and relatively uncommercialised islands on earth

5

06 November 2004 & 05 March 2005 21 nights
NOW from £2400 per person

Following two relaxing nights at one of our two hotels in Kenya you fly to Mahe, for three enchanting days in the Seychelles, the epitome of a tropical paradise. Two

10 lazy days at the sea bring you to Mauritius, renowned for its exquisite beaches, blue lagoons and coral reefs. Savour the French flair of neighbouring La Réunion, an island of dramatic volcanic craters and gorges, before rounding the coast of Madagascar to the 'Perfumed Isle'

15 of Nosy Be. Explore the lush plantations of the French Island of Mayotte and relax on the tiny atoll[1] of Mesali before calling at mysterious Zanzibar, little-changed since the days of Livingstone and Speke.

(From African Safari Club advertisement displayed in
***The Sunday Times* 04 January 2004)**

Note:
[1] A ring-shaped coral reef, enclosing a lagoon

Exercise 7.2

Read the advertisement for *An Indian Ocean Odyssey* and answer the following questions:

1. If you start your tour on 05 March, what date will it finish?

2. List all the adjectives which try to convince the reader that this would be an enjoyable holiday.

3. Why do you think the advertiser used the word 'Odyssey' instead of 'journey', 'expedition', 'tour', 'trip' or 'cruise'?

4. What is the minimum cost of this holiday for two people?

5. Which European country once governed most of the islands on this tour?

6. Find another word or words for (a) uncommercialised (line 3), (b) epitome (line 9) and (c) savour (line 12).

Exercise 7.3

Your turn to write:

1.   Write about any hot place that you have visited. Include what you saw, heard, smelt and tasted.

2.   Write a story about a child who has to make a new life a long way from his or her previous home

3.   Read one of the books listed in the 'Have you read?' section and write a review of it.

4.   The adder is Britain's only poisonous snake. Write an article for your school magazine about it. Do your research carefully. Include the adder's appearance, food, habits, how it breeds and where it is likely to be seen. Mention its potential danger too.

5.   Write a two- or three-paragraph advertisement for a newspaper or magazine to attract tourists to the area you live in.

6.   Imagine you are Flora. Write her diary for the first full day in her new home.

7.   Write a story called 'First Impressions.'

Grammar and punctuation

Conjunctions

Conjunctions are words such as 'and' and 'but' which link other words, sentences and ideas together. They form a junction or join.

For example:

Zebras **and** wildebeests roam the vast plains of Africa.

Egypt is a very hot country in summer **but** it's quite comfortable in winter.

We visited Dubai last summer **although** we weren't able to stay there long.

I don't want to visit Australia **because** I don't like the heat.

A conjunction linking two nouns together

Other examples of conjunctions are:

or	if	until
although	so	unless
as	before	after

Exercise 7.4

Conjunction activity:

A sentence which contains a single statement is called a **simple sentence**. Rewrite these pairs of simple sentences as one longer sentence using a conjunction. You may need to alter the words slightly.

e.g.   Giraffes are common in Kenya. Tourists can see them from safari vehicles.

*Giraffes are common in Kenya **so** tourists can see them from safari vehicles.*

1.   Tigers live in India. Lions are native to Africa.

2.   My little sister is hungry. We must have lunch soon.

3.   Dolphins are mammals. They swim like fish.

4.   We must hurry to the classroom. We shall be late.

5.   Ants live in colonies. They work together.

6.   A python is not dangerous to human beings. Don't interfere with it.

7.   It is very hot in Hong Kong. Most of the buildings are air-conditioned.

8.   Marcus is in the choir. His sister plays hockey for the school team.

Compound sentences

A longer sentence in which two or more ideas are hooked together by conjunctions is known as a **compound sentence**.

You can sometimes move the conjunction around in your sentence to change its shape. It is as if the sentence were being turned inside out.

*Bees buzz in and out of flowers **because** they need nectar.*

means almost the same as:

***Because** they need nectar, bees buzz in and out of flowers.*

And:

*Vultures feed on dead animals **although** they don't hunt and kill their own prey.*

means almost the same as:

***Although** they don't hunt and kill their own prey, vultures feed on dead animals.*

A conjunction moving around a sentence

Try occasionally turning a sentence inside out to add variety to your writing.

Exercise 7.5

Now for some practice with the names of marks of punctuation:

1. Do you remember all the punctuation words you've learned so far? Underline the punctuation words hidden in these sentences:

e.g.   Let's go and <u>question Mark.</u>

  (a) TV sit-com makes me laugh.
  (b) If Rop writes to Tessa, will Tessa post Rop her letter as she promised?
  (c) Could Ashley win the race?
  (d) 'I'm very shy,' Phenome explained.
  (e) You can see the petrol tank is full! Stop the pump!

2. Unscramble these letters. Each one makes a mark of punctuation.

  (a) mocma   (d) trackeb
  (b) shad   (e) pull soft
  (c) heapstroop   (f) tramesko quin

Vocabulary and spelling

1. **Aquamarine** means blue like sea water. Aqua comes from the Latin word for water (*aqua*) and marine comes from the Latin word for sea (*mare*).

  An **aquarium** is a tank of water in which fish are kept and an **aqueduct** is a bridge which carries a water supply across a valley or open space. An **aquatic** animal is one which lives in water and an **aqualung** is underwater breathing equipment for divers.

  Weston-super-Mare is a town in Somerset which is on the sea. The Royal **Marines** are a regiment of soldiers who specialise in working with or near the sea. **Mariner** is another word for a sailor

2. The word **punctuation** comes from the Latin word for a point. We put points – or full stops – and other marks in our sentences to make them clearer or more pointed.

  We get **puncture** from the same Latin word. Something which is punctured (a car tyre, for example) has been pricked with a point.

  A **punctual** person is someone who does everything on the dot or the precise point of time.

Exercise 7.6

Use these words in sentences of your own:

marine	aquatic	mariner
puncture	submarine	punctual

Exercise 7.7

These words all contain '-our':

neighbour	savour	colour
humour	flamour	saviour
favour	honour	labour

Write each of these words into short part-sentences. You can add extra letters if you need to. e.g. 'Our neighbour's dog', 'Sense of humour', 'Colouring book'. Try to think of several uses for each word. It will give you practice in writing them down correctly spelt.

Exercise 7.8

Look carefully at these words. They all have the letters 'gh' but they do not all sound alike or rhyme:

laugh	dough
plough	through
thorough	cough
daughter	borough
bough	brought

Work with a partner. Make sure you both know (a) how to say each word aloud and (b) how to write each down.

Speaking and listening

1. Think of somewhere that you've been on a day trip or on holiday. You have one minute to convince a partner that it would be worth visiting. Spend a few minutes working out in your mind what you're going to say before you start. Take it in turns to speak.

2. Choose a famous person, dead or alive. Find out what you can about him or her. Then pretend that you are that person and give a short talk about 'yourself' to the rest of the class. Ask the class to question you when you've finished talking.

3. Where in the world would you most like to go and why? Discuss your thoughts in a pair. Then join up with another pair. Take it in turns to tell the other pair not about your own but about your partner's travel ambitions. You will need to listen carefully to what he or she tells you to do this well!

Have you read?

All these stories are set across various continents in very hot places:

Other Echoes by Adèle Geras (David Flickling Books 2004)
Village by the Sea by Anita Desai (Puffin 2001)
Roll of Thunder, Hear My Cry by Mildred E Taylor (Puffin 1994)
Walkabout by James Vance Marshall (Puffin 1963)
Gold Dust by Geraldine McCaughrean (OUP 2004)
Journey to Jo Burg by Beverley Naidoo (Collins 1987)
When the World Began: Stories Collected in Ethiopia by Elizabeth Laird (OUP 2000)
Lion Country by Colin Dann (Hutchinson 2000)
Motherland by Vineeta Vijayaraghavan (Chicken House 2003)

And if you've done all that

● Look at an atlas. Find three cities in the tropics. Pick ones which are in different continents or a long way apart. Use the Internet to find out about the life and climate there. Prepare a short talk for the class about one of the three.

● Write a story based in one of the three tropical cities you have researched. Use what you have found out to make your writing colourful and believable. Convince your readers that you've been there!

● Find out who David Livingstone and John Speke were. Make a poster about them for the classroom wall.

Chapter 8

Traditional tales

Every culture has its folk, fairy or traditional stories which are passed down from adults to children. You will almost certainly know, for example, Cinderella and Red Riding Hood. Here's one from Egypt.

1   Uba-na-ner was a handsome and clever young man whose speciality was magic. And everything seemed to be going his way.

He was a great favourite of King Nebka, the Pharaoh of Egypt, who admired Uba-na-ner's skill as a magician. So the king gave the young man a large and elegant house
5   whose many windows and verandas looked across the great glassy River Nile.

Something else was making Uba-na-ner very happy too. He was engaged to marry a beautiful, young woman with glossy, dark hair and eyes like amber. He was looking forward to bringing her home to his riverside house and raising a family with her there.

Then his world fell apart. On the very day that he was to be married his pretty bride ran
10   away with another man!

Uba-na-ner was furious. For several days he shut himself away in his house unable to think straight. He wanted revenge. Eventually he thought of a plan.

The young magician fetched his box made of black ebony wood and held together by finely-wrought bands of gold and silver. This was where he kept his copies of some
15   ancient magic spells written on rolled-up papyrus.

After consulting the words on the scroll, Uba-na-ner took a piece of white wax. This he moulded in the warmth of his hands into the shape of a small white crocodile.

He breathed on his model and whispered some magic words. Suddenly the creature began to twitch, and it grew bigger and bigger. Soon it was a fearsome, thrashing
20   crocodile, huge with a long muzzle and ugly interlocking teeth. But it stayed as white as snow – like the wax it was made from.

'Fetch my enemy!' commanded Uba-na-ner. The gigantic white reptile swam powerfully away into the waters of the Nile.

Uba-na-ner knew that his former fiancée's husband would, sooner or later, bathe in the
25   Nile, and so it proved. A few days later the great white crocodile returned to Uba-na-ner with the hapless young man held tightly in its monstrous jaws.

'Kill him!' Uba-na-ner signalled. The crocodile disappeared back into the Nile and the young man was never seen again alive.

30 Clearly it was murder and it wasn't long before King Nebka got to hear about it. The bereaved bride went to see the King. She wept and wept, but she also told him who the murderer was.

Nebka was very upset. He liked Uba-na-ner and found it hard to believe that his favourite would do such a thing. Nevertheless he had to question the young magician.

35 Uba-na-ner denied nothing. Instead he led Nebka to the bank of the Nile and clapped his hands. The white crocodile reappeared at his summons, the dead man's body still in its mouth.

The King's attendants were very frightened. Never had they seen a Nile crocodile so colossal or so ruthless. But Nebka was calm and brave. And something about the king's tranquil courage made Uba-na-ner – at last – realise what a terrible thing he had done.

40 Regretting his action and feeling real remorse for the distress he had caused, Uba-na-ner made a quick movement with his hands. He said something which no one else understood. Instantly the big, muscular crocodile began to shrink. It stopped moving. Soon, as they watched, it had turned back into a small, white, wax figure.

45 In his house, Uba-na-ner went to the black, gold and silver casket and put the wax model safely inside with the papyrus scroll of magic spells.

Then he went to King Nebka, knelt before him and offered him the box, because he was truly sorry for what he had done.

'I think you really do regret your evil deed,' said the Pharaoh, 'so I will pardon you and you can remain one of my courtiers. However, you will never be allowed to have this
50 box again. It will remain hidden for ever in my palace.'

(Traditional Egyptian tale, retold by Susan Elkin)

Exercise 8.1

Read the traditional Egyptian tale above and then answer these questions as fully as you can:

1. Where, exactly, did Uba-na-ner keep the instructions for his spells?
2. Give another word or group of words which means the same as (a) revenge (line 12), (b) bereaved (line 30), (c) summons (line 35) and (d) remorse (line 40).
3. Describe the crocodile in your own words.
4. Explain in your own words as fully as can why Uba-na-ner was so upset on what would have been his wedding day.
5. Why did King Nebka show mercy to Uba-na-ner?

A traditional Egyptian recipe

Falafel is a traditional Egyptian food. It looks like tiny burgers but contains no meat. It is made from chickpeas (or other sorts of peas, beans or lentils) with spices. Office workers in Cairo buy freshly cooked falafel in rolls from kiosks and take-away shops at lunchtime. Here is a recipe, but do not try to make falafel yourself without adult help:

1
       1 large tin of chickpeas or lentils
       1 large onion, chopped into pieces
       1 teaspoonful ground coriander
       1 teaspoonful ground cumin
5
       1 clove of garlic, peeled and crushed (in a garlic press)
       A little salt and pepper (if you like it)
       A handful of wholemeal flour to dip the falafel in before cooking
       Vegetable oil for frying

Wash your hands. Get out all the ingredients.

10   Drain the chickpeas or lentils. Put all the ingredients except the flour and oil into a food processor or blender. Switch on and process until fairly smooth. Tip or scrape mixture into a bowl.

Use a tablespoon. Take a tablespoonful of the mixture in your (clean) hands. Roll it into a small flat cake. Dip the falafel in the flour and put it on a large plate. Do this until all
15   the mixture is used up.

Heat the oil in a frying pan. Fry the falafel gently until brown on both sides. Unless you have very large frying pan, you will probably need to cook the falafel in batches.

Falafel is tasty in rolls, baps or pitta bread; or try it with salad.

Exercise 8.2

Read the traditional Egyptian recipe on page 65 and answer the following questions:

1. Which two spices are used in falafel?
2. Explain in your own words why you will probably not be able to cook your falafel all at once.
3. Would you offer falafel to a vegetarian guest and, if so, why?
4. Where can you see falafel being eaten today?
5. You should always wash your hands before cooking but why is it particularly important when you're making falafel?
6. How can you tell that your falafel is cooked?

Exercise 8.3

Your turn to write:

1. Write a story about a crocodile or a magician (or both).
2. Make up a story about anything you wish with the title 'Revenge' or 'Remorse'.
3. Write a recipe for any food you know how to cook and like eating. You can include an introduction like the one to the falafel recipe if you wish.
4. Uba-na-ner's fiancée broke her promise to him because she fell in love with the man killed on Uba-na-ner's orders. Imagine you are her and write her story. You could write in the form of a diary if you wish.
5. Write in any way you choose about Egypt.
6. Write a description of a river you know well.
7. Write a review of any book which you have read recently.

Grammar and punctuation

Subjects and objects

The subject of a sentence, as you may know from your Latin lessons, is the person or thing which is 'doing the verb'. The object of a sentence is the person or thing which is affected by the action of the verb. In the following examples, the object is shown in bold:

Uba-na-ner fetched his **box**.
Wash your **hands**.
Office workers buy **falafel**.
He wanted **revenge**.

It is generally considered a bad thing to confuse a subject with an object, as the princess who found herself kissing the frog discovered – or was it the frog kissing the princess?

Exercise 8.4

Copy these sentences. Put a **green** rectangle round the subjects and a **red** oval round the objects:

1. A traditional tale affects many readers.

2. Falafel makes fingers sticky.

3. Uba-na-ner watched the big crocodile.

4. King Nebka forgave Uba-na-ner.

5. Nicola ate her falafel.

The passive voice

You can often reverse the subject and object in a sentence by adjusting the words and using 'by'. If the verb is in the **active** voice, the subject of the sentence 'does' the verb to the object. If the verb is in the **passive** voice, the action of the verb is 'done' to the subject **by** someone or something.

e.g. The king **rules** his country (active voice).

The country **is ruled by** its king (passive voice).

Exercise 8.5

1. Rewrite the five sentences in Exercise 8.4 in the passive voice.

2. Practise writing sentences in the active and passive. Begin with these words:
   (a) Uba-na-ner's fiancée . . .
   (b) My cooking . . .
   (c) Take-away shops in Cairo . . .
   (d) Falafel . . .
   (e) A piece of white wax . . .
   (f) The magician . . .
   (g) Crocodiles . . .
   (h) Egyptians . . .

3. Provide subjects for these objects to form sentences. You will need a verb as well:
   (a) . . . the story.
   (b) . . . the River Nile.
   (c) . . . bad behaviour.
   (d) . . . the smell of falafel frying.
   (e) . . . Uba-na-ner.
   (f) . . . magic spells.

Colons

The colon (:) means 'as follows' or 'like this'. It's useful when you want to introduce a list or some information in your writing. Sometimes it is used to introduce what someone says, too.

For example:

> Here are some examples of traditional stories: Rumpelstiltskin, Alibaba and the Forty Thieves, The Three Little Pigs and Brer Rabbit.

> You make falafel like this: mix up the ingredients, form cakes and fry them.

> King Nebka said: 'I will forgive you.'

A colon

Exercise 8.6

1. Write three sentences including lists in which the list is preceded by a colon. Your sentences can be about anything you like.

2. Make up three sentences containing the words 'like this', 'as follows', 'thus', 'in the following way' or 'for example'. Use a colon to link the next part of the sentence.

3. Compose three sentences in which a colon comes before speech.

(Did you know that Colon is also a town in Panama, in central America?)

Vocabulary and spelling

1. If you are **engaged** to someone, it means that you have agreed to marry him or her. English often has several words which mean almost the same thing. 'Espoused', 'betrothed', 'affianced', 'tokened', 'promised' and 'plighted' all mean the same as 'engaged', although some of these are rather old-fashioned words which you will probably see only in books written long in the past.

   Words which are similar in meaning are called 'synonyms'.

   How many synonyms can you think of, or find in a dictionary, for (a) colossal, (b) frightened and (c) meal?

   A thesaurus is a special sort of dictionary which lists groups of synonyms. You can access a dictionary or thesaurus on most computers as well as by using books.

2. **Ruthless** means without mercy or pity. 'Ruth' is an old English word which means mercy. It is now very rarely used other than as part of the word 'ruthless' and in the female name Ruth. Words which have died out – or almost died out – of the language are called 'archaisms'.

Do you know, or can you find out, what the following female names mean? They are all archaisms, or unusual words in English:

Felicity
Verity
Carol
Sally
Mavis

3. Many words in English end in '–ss' as well as the ones ending '-ness' which we looked at in Chapter 5.

Some nouns and verbs such as 'distress', 'address' and 'process' use the double 'ss' for emphasis because the second half of the word is accented. Practise saying these and think of other examples.

When a noun ending in 'ss' becomes plural, or the word is a part of the verb which needs 's', it takes '–es'. So: distresses, addresses and processes.

Some nouns – princess, actress, mayoress – end in '–ess' because they are the feminine form of other words such as prince, actor and mayor. How many other examples can you think of? Be careful with these. They too need **-es** when they are plural and **-'s** when they are possessive. So: three actresses; the mayoress's son.

Then there are adjectives which end in '–less' such as 'ruthless', 'harmless' and 'careless'. They take 'ly' when they become adverbs. So: 'ruthlessly', 'harmlessly' and 'carelessly'.

Learn the spelling of these:

confess	discuss
countess's (daughter)	useless
depress	endless
expresses	possesses
progress	(six) princesses
princess's (shoe)	tirelessly
hopeless	effortlessly
needless	wireless
compresses	goddesses
lioness's (tail)	success

A puzzle:

Which word can be changed from masculine and plural to feminine and singular by adding 's'? The solution can be obtained from the publishers, for a small fee!

Speaking and listening

1. Work with a partner on a traditional story which you both know well (or choose one from one of the books in the 'Have you read?' section). Practise telling it together, taking turns to speak in order to make your version of it as dramatic and interesting as you can. Perform your story for the rest of the class.

2. Working in a group, play 'Pass the Story'. One of you begins a story. After one or two sentences the first person stops, possibly mid-sentence. The next person in the group continues the story and then in turn passes it on. You can also play 'Pass the Story' by saying just one word each and seeing how the story develops.

3. Prepare a short talk about your favourite food or recipe. Give your talk in front of a group or class.

4. In groups, talk about animals in stories. Why are some always bad and some always good? Think of examples. Are those animals really like that in nature? Do you like to read about animals in stories? If so why, or if not, why not?

5. Interview someone who has been to Egypt. Write an article based on your interview for the school or class magazine.

Have you read?

These books contain a wide range of traditional stories from all over the world:

The Old Stories: Folk Tales from East Anglia and the Fen Country by Kevin Crossley-Holland, (Orion 1999)

Why the Fish Laughed and Other Tales by Kevin Crossley-Holland (OUP 2002)

Tales of Ancient Persia by Barbara Leonie Picard (OUP 1972)

Hero Tales From the British Isles by Barbara Leonie Picard (OUP 1966)

Folk Tales for Reading and Telling by Leila Berg (Macmillan 1976)

English Fairy Tales edited by Flora Annie Steel and illustrated by Arthur Rackham (Wordsworth Children's Classics 1994)

The Adventures of Robin Hood by Roger Lancelyn Green (Puffin Classics 1995)

Tales of Ancient Egypt by Roger Lancelyn Green (Puffin 1970)

Hans Andersen's Fairy Tales (Oxford World Classics 1998)

Jamil's Clever Cat: A Bengali Folk Tale by Fiona French (Frances Lincoln Ltd 1999)

Mariana and the Merchild: A Folk Tale from Chile by Caroline Pitcher (Frances Lincoln Ltd 2001)

The Boy Who Drew Cats and Other Japanese Fairy Tales by L Hearn (Dover Publications 1998)

Stories from Around the World by H Amery (Usborne Publications Ltd 2000)

And if you've done all that

- Collect traditional recipes from around the world. Use the Internet, cookery books or ask people you know. Create a global cookery booklet. Ideally, you should try out the recipes. You may find you have to edit or rewrite some of them to make the meaning clear. It may also be necessary to suggest slightly different ingredients if the recipe includes items which you can't buy easily in Britain. Can you sell your booklet to raise money for one of the charities which helps starving people in poor countries?

- Make a large map of Egypt as a poster for the classroom. Show the River Nile and all the major cities. What other information can you get onto it?

- Prepare a short talk for the class about the Ancient Egyptians. Include how they lived, what they believed and what they did. Use a computer program such as *Powerpoint* to illustrate your talk.

- Find out about the Suez Canal. Where is it, why was it built, by whom and why is (or was) it important?

Chapter 9

Dealing with disability

Alan Marshall, who grew up in Queensland, Australia, caught polio in 1908 when he was six. The disease left him permanently paralysed in the legs – especially his right leg – and unable to walk without crutches. He died in 1984.

1   My crutches were gradually becoming part of me. I had developed arms out of proportion to the rest of my body and my armpits were now tough and hard. The crutches did not chafe me any more and I could walk without discomfort.

I practised different walking styles, calling them by the names applied to the gaits of
5   horses. I could trot, pace, canter and gallop. I fell frequently and heavily but learned to throw myself into positions that saved my bad leg from injury. I typed the falls I had and when beginning to fall always knew whether it would be a 'bad' or a 'good' fall. If both crutches slipped backwards when I was well advanced on my forward swing I fell backwards and this was the worst fall of all since it often resulted in my being winded or
10   twisting my bad leg beneath me. It was a painful fall and I used to thump the earth with my hands to keep from crying out when I fell in this manner. When only one crutch slipped or stuck a stone or root, I fell forward on to my hands and was never hurt.

I was never free of bruises or lumps or gravel rashes and every evening found me attending to some injury I had received that day.

15   But they did not distress me. I accepted these inconveniences as being part of normal living and I never for a moment regarded them as a result of being crippled, a state which, at this period, I never applied to myself.

I began walking to school and became acquainted with exhaustion – the state so familiar to cripples and their constant concern.

20   I always cut corners, always made in as straight a line as I could to go where I wanted to go. I would walk through clumps of thistles rather than go round them and climb through fences rather than deviate a few yards to go through a gate.

Joe Carmichael and I hunted rabbits and hares together. We went tramping through the bush and across open paddocks with a pack of dogs. When we roused the hare and the
25   dogs gave chase I watched with keen pleasure the kangaroo dog's undulating run, his lowered head close to the ground, the magnificent curve of his neck and shoulders and the swinging, leaning turn of him as he came round after the dodging hare.

After tea, before it was time to go to bed, in that first expectant darkness when the frogs

30 from the swamp began their chirping and the early possums peered out from hollows, I would stand at the gate. In my imagination I would launch myself into a powerful run through the night like an animal. As a dog racing through the night, I experienced no effort, no fatigue and no painful falls.

But I didn't resent my crutches. I could not feel that way. I left them behind in my dreams but I returned to them without resentment.

(Adapted from *I Can Jump Puddles* by Alan Marshall)

Exercise 9.1

Read the extract from *I Can Jump Puddles* and then answer these questions:

1. Why were some falls more serious than others?

2. Why do you think Alan Marshall describes the hunting dog's movements in such detail?

3. How can you tell that Alan Marshall does not feel sorry for himself?

4. Give another word or short phrase which means the same as (a) chafe (line 3), (b) deviate (line 22), (c) undulating (line 25) and (d) expectant (line 28).

5. List all the details which tell you that the setting for this story is Australia.

6. Explain what Alan Marshall means by 'I always cut corners' (line 20). Why do you think he did this?

Bones and muscles

1   Your skeleton is a scaffolding of more than 200 living bones. It supports you and keeps you upright. The skeleton may seem fragile, but it carries the whole weight of the body. Your muscles are attached to the bony scaffolding. They pull on the bones to make you move.

5   The word skeleton comes from a Greek word meaning 'dried up', but bones are not dry and brittle. Bones are alive. They grow as we do, repair themselves if they are broken and become stronger as we exercise. A living bone has layers of hard calcium phosphate on the outside and a honeycomb of hard bone and living cells within. This makes it strong and light.

10   Most organs of the body are soft and delicate. Our bones protect these soft organs from injury. The skull bones, for example, fit tightly together to form a tough case for the brain. The ribs form a rigid case around the lungs and heart and the hip bones enclose the bladder and intestines.

The longest bone in your body is your thigh bone (femur). Your smallest bone is in your ear. It is about the size of a grain of rice.

(From *The Young Oxford Encyclopaedia of Science*)

Exercise 9.2

Read the passage about bones and muscles and then answer these questions:

1.   Give other words for (a) scaffolding (line 1), (b) rigid (line 11) and (c) femur (line 13).

2.   What are the skeleton's three main jobs?

3.   Explain in your own words why the name 'skeleton' (line 4) is inappropriate.

4.   Which substance gives bones their strength?

5.   How many bones (roughly) do all the pupils in your class have amongst them?

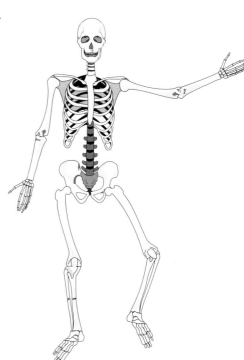

Exercise 9.3

Your turn to write:

1. Write a letter to a newspaper or magazine arguing for better facilities for disabled people.

2. Write about skeletons in any way you wish.

3. Imagine that you are unable to walk. Write a story about your life.

4. Write a story about someone who is without one of the senses (sight, hearing, smell, taste or touch) and who then has an operation which gives him or her that sense.

5. Take the title 'Walk'. Write a story, a personal account, a description, your thoughts and feelings or anything else which the title suggests to you.

6. Write about a disabled person that you know.

Grammar and punctuation

Pronouns

A pronoun is a word which takes the place of a noun. There are several types, and we begin with **personal pronouns**. These are:

	Singular	Plural
1st person	I	we
2nd person	you	you
3rd person	he, she, it	they

A personal pronoun

For example:

My dog is called Sheba and he likes bones. ('He' is a pronoun used instead of 'dog' or 'Sheba'.)

I like apple pie and it is best with custard. ('It' is used instead of repeating 'apple pie'.)

All the children in my class are excited about the trip to Windsor because they are all looking forward to seeing the castle. ('They' means 'all the children in my class'.)

Possessive pronouns tell you who or what something belongs to:

	Singular	Plural
1st person	my	our
2nd person	your	your
3rd person	his, her, its	their

For example:

my coat, his book, their car, our mother.

A possessive pronoun

Notice also these forms:

	Singular	Plural
1st person	mine	ours
2nd person	yours	yours
3rd person	his, hers, its	theirs

For example:

> That pen is mine (it means 'That pen is my pen'.)
> That house is theirs (it means 'That house is their house'.)

Possessive pronouns (see note at end of chapter) NEVER need an apostrophe. So remember that:

> **Its** means belonging to it.
> **It's** means 'it is' or 'it has'. The apostrophe stands for the missing letters.

Exercise 9.4

Rewrite these sentences using pronouns where necessary to avoid repeating the nouns:

1. The children protested when the children were told off.

2. Emma's father asked Emma to help her disabled brother.

3. The headmaster asked the teachers to come to the headmaster's office when the teachers had dismissed their classes.

4. The mayoress said that the mayoress had a severe headache.

5. The blind man said that the blind man used a guide dog.

6. Raj took one look at the calculator and saw that it was Raj's.

Exercise 9.5

Shorten these sentences by using a possessive pronoun:

For example:

> Original sentence: This cat belongs to us. (5 words)
> Rewritten sentence: This cat is ours. (4 words)

1. The new caravan is their property.

2. Does the red scarf belong to her?

3. This wheelchair belongs to me.

4. You must take the responsibility.

5. This is the home which we own.

Exercise 9.6

Put **its** or **it's** in the gaps in the following sentences:

1. --- a pity that --- raining today.

2. The skeleton in the science lab has lost --- labels.

3. What a long day --- been.

4. --- necessary to visit a museum to find out about --- history.

5. Ask anyone in the school to tell you about --- rules.

Pronouns in the accusative

Very few words in English change their form depending on the part that they are playing in a sentence; but pronouns do. Take care, for example, with the pronouns 'me' and 'I', especially in sentences where they are used with another noun or pronoun.

So, here are all the personal pronouns again, this time in the accusative case, which we use when they are the object of the sentence or after a preposition:

	Singular	**Plural**
1st person	me	us
2nd person	you	you
3rd person	him, her, it	them

For example:

> He and I are going to play cricket (because you would say 'He is going to play cricket' or 'I am going to play cricket').

> Mr Baker gave him and me a detention (because you would say 'Mr Baker gave him a detention' and 'Mr Baker gave me a detention').

> He is going to play with you and me ('you' and 'me' used after the preposition 'with').

Exercise 9.7

Put pronouns in these sentences:

1. Perry and --- are going to learn the names of all the bones in the body.

2. Jasmine, who is profoundly deaf, invited Ella and --- to her party.

3. There was trouble ahead for Guy and ---.

4. Uncle John sent presents for James and ---.

5. Clearly Felix and --- were in trouble because he had lost his crutches.

6. Mrs Burns grumbled at Jake and --- for being late.

Inverted commas

Inverted commas (" " or ' ') are used to separate the words that someone is speaking from other words in a piece of writing. They are sometimes called speech marks or quotation marks. They always come in pairs at the beginning and end of the words spoken.

They can be single or double. The normal convention is to use single inverted commas, unless there is a need to open inverted commas inside a passage that is already in inverted commas, in which case that passage goes in double inverted commas (but you may find it the other way round).

For example:

'Peter,' I asked, 'how many times have I said "No" to you today?'

or:

"Peter," I asked, "how many times have I said 'No' to you today?"

A pair of inverted commas

Exercise 9.8

Put inverted commas in the correct places in these sentences:

1.   Is it morning already? asked Joshua, sitting up in bed.

2.   Oh please let me go, pleaded Peter.

3.   Dad announced: As soon as Mrs Methuen says Good morning I shall be going out.

4.   Do you know, said Jack, that the collar bone is called the clavicle?

5.   My address, said Mr Micawber, is Windsor Terrace, City Road.

The exact words that someone speaks, enclosed in inverted commas, is known as direct speech.

Vocabulary and spelling

Words which are opposite in meaning are called **antonyms**.

So 'weak' is an antonym for 'strong', 'backward' for 'forward' and 'curved' for 'straight'.

Sometimes you can think of several antonyms for one word, particularly if that word has more than one meaning.

For example: antonyms for 'deep' could include 'shallow', 'insincere', 'straightforward', 'light' and 'thin' because the adjective 'deep' means a number of different things.

Exercise 9.9

How many antonyms can you think of for the following adjectives?

1. simple
2. easy
3. sad

4. bright
5. dark
6. funny

A thesaurus might help you with this.

Spelling

In the extract from *I Can Jump Puddles* on page 72, Alan Marshall uses the word 'frequently' (line 5). Check that you know the meanings and spellings of the following words which include 'qu':

eloquent
quizzical
acquiesce
equine
quartz

query
quadruped
aquatic
sequence
antique

In words which come from Ancient Greek the 'f' sound is often written as 'ph' – as in the word 'phosphate' – which is a particularly good example as it has 'ph' twice. Check that you know the meanings and spellings of the following words which include a 'ph':

typhoon
physical
emphasise
prophet
philosopher

symphony
xylophone
triumphant
catastrophe
sphinx

Speaking and listening

1. Tell the class about any disabled person you know. It might be a member of your family, a friend or someone in your community. The person could be blind, deaf, have walking difficulties, be mentally handicapped or have any other sort of disability.

2. Work in pairs. Talk about how suitable your school is for people – pupils and adults – with various sorts of disability. Make a list of possible improvements. Put all the lists on a notice board and use them as the basis of a class discussion.

3. Prepare a short talk for the class about the work of one of the charities which works with disabled people – Guide Dogs for the Blind, Scope or Mencap for example, but there are many other possibilities.

Have you read?

These books are by, or partly about, people who have overcome disabilities. Some are fictional and some are autobiographical – factual accounts of people's experiences.

I Can Jump Puddles by Alan Marshall (Puffin Plus 1989)
Good Vibrations: My Biography Evelyn Glennie (Hutchison 1990)
Northern Lights by Anne College (Piper's Ash 2001)
My Left Foot by Christy Brown (Minerva 1990)
Emma and I by Sheila Hocken (Time Warner 1993)
The Curious Incident Of The Dog in the Night-Time by Mark Haddon (Jonathan Cape 2003)
Heidi by Johanna Spyri (Penguin Modern Classics 1995)
Flowers for Algernon by Daniel Keyes (Gollancz 2000)
The Illustrated Mum by Jacqueline Wilson (Corgi Children's Paperback 2000)

And if you've done all that

- Read some of the books in the 'Have you read?' section. Write reviews of them. Focus on what you have learned about the disability in question.

- Design a classroom which would meet the needs of as many different sorts of disabled pupil as you can. Use a computer or sketch your design by hand. It will probably need some notes of explanation. Display your work in the classroom.

- Get permission from your teacher to contact a disabled person by letter, e-mail or telephone according to what is appropriate and/or practicable for him or her to use. See if you can invite him or her to school to talk to pupils about his or her experiences.

- Find out the names of as many bones in the body as possible. Create a comic poem or song using as many of these words as you can.

A note on possessive pronouns

It is easy to mistake possessive pronouns for adjectives because, after all, they seem to behave like adjectives by qualifying nouns – **his book, their mother, our house**. But they are pronouns because they are a different grammatical form – the genitive as you may know from your Latin – of personal pronouns such as **he, they** or **we**.

Randolph Quirk, a very famous and great grammarian, also points out that adjectives are different from possessive pronouns because you can use adjectives in lists, but possessive pronouns can be used only one at a time. For example, in a phrase such as 'his strong, brown, friendly dog barks' you can use three adjectives ('strong', 'brown' and 'friendly') but only one possessive pronoun ('his'). If you or your teacher wants to know more about this, look at *Comprehensive Grammar of the English Language* by Raldolph Quirk, Sidney Greenbaum, Geoffrey Leech and Jan Svartvik (1985 Longman) section 6.29.

Chapter 10

Sports

Billy, the central character in this story, is over 80 but before he got caught up in the Second World War, he was a Chelsea Football Club player. He is reliving his memories.

1   The first match I ever played for Chelsea Reserves was against Arsenal Reserves. There weren't many to watch but Mum came and Joe and Emmy and Ossie and they saw me score two goals. One was a simple enough tap-in. The other I really enjoyed: a dribble in towards goal, slipping the ball through the legs of one defender, round another and a

5   little chip over the goalie. I can still see the look on his face as the ball floated over his head and into the goal – horror, disbelief, despair all in one. Lovely!

    I was in the newspapers the following day: 'Billy the Kid bamboozles the Arsenal.' For the whole of the next year I was a regular in the Chelsea Reserves, and a regular in the newspapers too. I didn't think life could get any better. But it did – for a while at least.

10   1939 began as the best year of my life. Towards the end of that football season I was picked for the first team. 12th March 1939, just a month or so before my nineteenth birthday, I trotted out in my Chelsea shirt for the first time. I was on cloud nine, seventh heaven. We were playing Preston North End away, and we lost badly. No one was looking at me, that was for sure. I was awful, leaden-legged and useless. Ossie, who

15   came to all my matches, took me on one side afterwards and said I had to forget the shirt, forget who I was playing for, where I was playing, all that, and just play the game.

    When we played Sunderland the next week at home, it was like I was in the playground again at school, or out in the park with Joe. I ran rings round them, laid on a couple of goals and scored one myself. That was the first time I heard the crowd at the Shed End

20   chanting my name – 'Billy, Billy the Kid! Billy, Billy the Kid!' It sends warm tingles up my spine even now just to think of it. Before the season ended three weeks later I had scored seven more goals and all the papers were saying I'd be playing for England before the end of the year. One paper called me 'Billy the Wonder Kid'. Another said I was as good as Stanley Matthews, maybe better. It would have gone to my head a lot

25   worse if it hadn't been for Ossie.

    'Don't read all that stuff, Billy,' he told me. 'Don't even look at it. Not good for you. Let your mum cut it out and stick it in a scrapbook. You can read it later when you're older – can't hurt you then.'

    Mum did put it all in a scrapbook – she was always taking it out and looking at it and

30   showing it – but it disappeared like everything else.

That summer, Mum married again, married Ossie – and I never even saw it coming. Joe and I were both 'best men' and Emmy was the bridesmaid. So the man who had taught me most of my football, who had been like a father to me since Dad died and a real
35   friend to the family, became my second father. It was a great day for all of us, confetti everywhere and a huge wedding cake made like a football pitch in Chelsea-blue icing. And then they went off to Broadstairs for a week's honeymoon.

They were still away on the third of September when war was declared – another thing I hadn't seen coming. I'd been too busy with my football to worry about what was going
40   on in the world outside.

(From *Billy the Kid* by Michael Morpurgo)

Exercise 10.1

Read the extract from *Billy the Kid* and then answer the following questions:

1. What were the approximate dates of (a) Billy's nineteenth birthday and (b) his mother's wedding?

2. Explain in as much detail as you can who you think Ossie is.

3. Why did Ossie tell Billy not to read newspaper accounts of his matches?

4. Why did Billy need to 'forget the shirt' (lines 15-16)?

5. How did Billy feel when he scored his first two goals against Arsenal Reserves?

6. What colour was a Chelsea shirt at this time?

7. How can you tell from this passage that Billy didn't go on being as happy as this?

Australia 17 – England 20

1	England won the Rugby World Cup with a breathtaking Jonny Wilkinson drop-goal[1] just 26 seconds from the end of a thrilling final in Sydney. Millions watched around the world as captain Martin Johnson became the first player to lead a northern-hemisphere side to the world title. Australia battled hard and were never out of the game but

5	ultimately fell just short, despite opening the scoring through wing Lote Tuqiri. The Wallabies started strongly when Tuqiri out-jumped Jason Robinson to a huge Stephen Larkham bomb with just six minutes on the clock. The score was no more than Australia deserved, but three Wilkinson penalties soon silenced the strong home support. Despite the rain continuing to fall, both sides chose to keep the ball in hand and, as the game

10	progressed, so the mighty England pack began to dominate.With just 10 minutes of the first half left, Ben Kay knocked-on[2] with the line beckoning, to the frustration of the visiting fans. Minutes later, England finally silenced their critics when Robinson scuttled over wide on the left after a powerful midfield burst from Lawrence Dallaglio.

	The men in white started the second half as they had finished the first. Johnson led from

15	the front with a towering performance and Dallaglio and flanker Richard Hill caused numerous problems down the middle of the pitch. However, just as England looked likely to pull away, two sloppy penalties allowed Elton Flatley to bring his side back within touching distance. England looked the more confident side with the ball in hand – but only just. Will Greenwood knocked on inside the Aussie 22 and Wilkinson then

20	missed a drop goal as the match entered a tense closing quarter. Runs from the powerful Stirling Mortlock and George Smith pushed England back into their own half, and as referee André Watson prepared to blow for full time, Flatley slotted his third kick of the half to push the match into extra time. The players looked understandably exhausted and, when Wilkinson and Flatley again swapped penalties, the match looked as if it was

25	heading into sudden death. England, however, were not to be denied and it was fitting that Wilkinson sealed a deserved victory as well as the most memorable result in English rugby history.

(Adapted from news.bbc.co.uk 23 November 2003)

Notes:
[1] A drop goal is where a player kicks the rugby ball over the cross bar and between the upright posts
[2] A knock-on is where a player knocks the rugby ball forward with his hands

Exercise 10.2

Read the extract from the BBC news report above and then answer the following questions:

1.	Who scored the winning goal?
2.	Name three other England players.
3.	Why did the match run to extra time?
4.	Explain in your own words what happened to make this an exceptionally exciting match.
5.	Which side does the writer support? Pick three separate words or phrases which make this clear.

Exercise 10.3

Your turn to write:

1. Write an account of a school match – any sport – for the school magazine.
2. Write a story entitled 'Goal'.
3. Write a story which includes the words 'I didn't think we'd ever win but . . .'.
4. Write a diary entry for someone who used to be a professional sportsman or woman a long time ago.
5. Write about sport in any way you wish.
6. Do you think there should be more or less sport played in schools? Why? Write your views.

Grammar and punctuation

Agreement of subject and verb

The pronouns 'I', 'he', 'she' and 'it'; words which end with '-one' (such as 'no one', 'none', 'anyone', 'everyone'); and words which end with '-body' (such as 'everybody', 'anybody', 'nobody' and 'somebody') are all **singular** words. Only one person or thing is involved.

The words 'we', 'they', 'people' and 'most' are **plural** words. More than one person or thing is involved.

Verbs must match – or agree with – the nouns they belong to:

Singular	Plural
I was	We were
She was	They were
No one was	People were
Everybody was	All were

Verbs agreeing with nouns

Exercise 10.4

Put 'was' or 'were' into the gaps in this passage:

We ----- waiting for the bus. We didn't mind whether it ----- a red, green or blue bus. We ----- prepared to take the first one which came. The centre of town ----- our destination. My eldest sister ----- going to a wedding and she ----- planning to buy a really special outfit. Determined as she ----- to buy something extravagant and colourful, we ----- sure that she would buy something black and dreary, because that's what she always does. However, none of us ----- right.

She eventually chose a bright pink suit, which she ----- going to wear with a lime green blouse and scarlet hat. Everybody ----- trying to dissuade her, but unfortunately we ----- unsuccessful. She ----- all set to go to the wedding looking like a parrot.

Collective nouns

A collective noun is a group word such as 'team' or 'side', both of which mean a group of players in a sport. Words like 'flock' (of birds) 'pack' (of wolves or cards) and 'clutch' (of eggs in a nest) are collective nouns too.

You have to be especially careful with the verbs when you're using collective nouns. Collective nouns are **singular**.

You should write:

> The herd of cows **was** brown and white.
> **Was** the baseball team dressed in bright colours?
> The audience **was** waving thousands of red, white and blue flags.

If, however, the subject is just 'cows', 'baseball players' or 'audience members', then these are **plural** because you are not using a collective noun. Remember: one team (singular); eleven players (plural).

A collection of collective nouns

Exercise 10.5

Match up these collective nouns with the common nouns they refer to:

1.	fleet	(a)	singers
2.	host	(b)	bells
3.	chest	(c)	ships
4.	swarm	(d)	grapes
5.	peal	(e)	angels
6.	gang	(f)	insects
7.	choir	(g)	drawers
8.	bunch	(h)	thieves

Exercise 10.6

Write out these sentences using the right form of the verb (in the present tense):

1. The hockey team --- triumphant after its win.
2. The hockey players --- nervous about their match.
3. Everyone in the team --- delighted.
4. The school's swimming relay team --- looking forward to the gala.
5. --- the musicians confident about the concert?
6. The wolf pack --- howling.
7. The choir --- on top form.
8. Everybody --- pleased.

Semicolons

A semicolon (;) can be used to separate items in a list where the list is too complicated and the sentence too long for commas to be strong enough. A semicolon is stronger than a comma.

Look at this sentence:

'In our school we play football, hockey, baseball, tennis, cricket and rounders.'

That is correct (see Chapter 3).

But suppose that you want to add additional information about each sport within a single long sentence:

In our school we play football, very popular with the boys, because we have extensive playing fields; hockey, loved by both boys and girls now that we have an all weather pitch; tennis, which works well because Mr Jonas, our tennis coach, is such an expert; cricket, although girls are not too keen; and rounders, which is a wonderful, all round game for pupils who aren't all that fond of sport.

A semicolon

The four semicolons are used to divide the main items on the list. Commas come between the semicolons to break up the additional information.

Exercise 10.7

Extend these sentences by giving more information about each of the sports mentioned, using semicolons:

1. My sister plays squash, badminton, tennis and table tennis.

2. The most popular sports on television are football, tennis, cricket and snooker.

3. I like swimming, ice-skating, ballet and riding.

Vocabulary and spelling

1. A **referee** (note the double 'ee' at the end) is someone who is referred to for a decision in a sports match. An **employee** is someone who is employed. A **nominee** is someone who is nominated (named or chosen).

   New words (neologisms) are sometime made up using patterns like these. Teachers now often refer to the pupils in their tutor group or form as **tutees**. A more experienced person who advises someone less experienced is called a 'mentor'. He or she might call the person being helped a **mentee**.

2. **Hemisphere** means half the world. It comes from the Greek words meaning 'half' and 'ball-shaped'. **Hemialgia** is pain limited to one side of the body and a **hemistitch** is half

a line of verse. A **hemidemisemiquaver** is a musical term meaning half of a half of a half of a semibreve – four full beats. You hold a hemidemisemiquaver for one sixty-fourth of a semibreve; no wonder musicians are often also good at maths!

Check that you know the spellings of these words, all taken from the two passages which open this chapter:

confetti	ultimately
disappeared	deserved
nineteenth	penalties
beckoning	disbelief
numerous	exhausted

To, two and too

Look carefully at these sentences:

> Rugby is one of **two** sports which are **too** good **to** miss.
> I know you are going **to** the **two** matches so can I come **too**?
> I want **to** play **two** games **too**.

Two: the number which comes between one and three.
Too: an adverb meaning too much. It also means 'as well'.
To: either a place word (preposition) as in 'to the match' or part of a verb as in 'to miss'.

Exercise 10.8

Write out these sentences putting two, too or to into the spaces:

1.   Our first eleven beat Millford School by --- goals --- one.

2.   It was --- hot even --- play tennis so we sat and ate --- ice creams each.

3.   --- boys played --- girls at table tennis in a game which the boys were surprised --- lose.

4.   Lacrosse is popular but lots of pupils like hockey ---.

5.   I am going --- work on cricketing skills this year, especially bowling.

6.   My --- friends and I have all been chosen --- swim for the school.

Speaking and listening

1.   Find out about a sport that you've never played and know nothing about. Give a short talk to the class about its history, rules and how and where it's played.

2.   Some adults think that sport, especially when it's played in teams, makes young people too competitive and is therefore not a good thing. Discuss this in a group. Try to consider all sides of the argument. Think of reasons why sport benefits young people and think of arguments against it.

3.   Work with a partner. Tell him or her about your favourite sport and why you like it, making sure you each have a different one (so you may need to choose your partner with care). Sport could include dance, gymnastics and athletics. Listen very carefully to your partner. Then join up with another pair. Take turns to tell the other pair, not about your own, but about your partner's sport.

Have you read?

These books are all about sport:

Billy the Kid by Michael Morpurgo (Collins 2002)
Goalkeepers are Different by Brian Glanville (Puffin 1993)
Down the Wicket by Bob Cattell (Red Fox 2001)
Bend It Like Beckham by Narinder Dhami (Hodder Children's Books 2002)
Ganging Up by Alan Gibbons (Orion 1996)
Together on Ice by Nicholas Walker (Macmillan Children's Books 1995)
The Transfer by Terence Blacker (Macmillan Children's Books 2001)
Quidditch Through the Ages: Comic Relief Edition by JK Rowling (Bloomsbury 2001)
Darcey Bussell's Favourite Ballet Stories (Red Fox 2002)
Gala Star by Ruth Dowley (Hodder Wayland 2001)
One Good Horse by Michael Hardcastle (Orion 1995)
Death Vault by Keith Miles (Lions Paperback 1990)
Mission Buffalo by Felice Arena (Collins 1997)
Football Fever edited by Tony Bradman (Corgi Children's Paperback 2000)
A Book of Two Halves edited by Nicholas Royle (Orion 1997)

And if you've done all that

- Football Association teams often have mysterious names such as Sheffield Wednesday, Tottenham Hotspur, Wolverhampton Wanderers and so on. Do you know why Arsenal players are nicknamed 'the Gunners'? Find out how and when some of these teams got their names. The clubs themselves may help you if you contact them and/or there may be information on the Internet.

- Research and write a short essay-length biography of a sporting hero or heroine from the past: WG Grace, Stanley Matthews, Roger Bannister, Kitty Godfrey – for example.

- In her *Harry Potter* books, JK Rowling devises Quidditch, a completely new sport for her young wizards and witches to play on broomsticks. Can you devise a fictional sport, complete with rules?